Once you understand your iniquity and carnality,
you will appreciate repentance (an attribute of God's amazing grace) all the more.

The WISDOM of The JUST

Endorsements

"It is my joy and privilege to recommend to you the writings of my good friend, Ed Marr. I was privileged to be his pastor for many years. During that time I saw in him the person that enjoyed getting into the Scripture and how it could be applied to the time in which we are living. Many were blessed as he would share the teachings that were so applicable to their lives.

"He has been in demand to share his insights into the Word, and I know you will be blessed as you read what God has put in his heart to share with you. As a friend and a student of the Word, I know you will find joy and inspiration in what he has shared relating to this hour in which we live, and I know you will be enriched."

Dr Dwaine E. Lee
Founder
Global Pastors, Inc.

***

"Ed Marr is a scholar with a keen sense of insight that is a God given gift. You will discover as you read this book that it is more than just another book ...but rather a gift of knowledge with the touch of divinity. A God-given book of information and inspiration.

"I have enjoyed the friendship of this gifted author for many years. He is a gentle giant with a passion for truth, and a compassion for mankind to experience real revelation. In a day of fake news and false doctrine his writings are like a cup of cool clean water to a thirsty soul. So get ready to be blessed ...refreshed ...and challenged and changed as you read his newest release ...l commend and recommend this new book!"

John Davis
Revivalist
Ambassador for the Brownsville Revival (Pensacola Outpouring)
under Pastor John Kilpatrick and Evangelist Steve Hill

***

"In this time of troubled waters, my good friend Ed Marr is unafraid to step out of the boat of religiousity and run to Jesus. Over the years that I have known Ed, I've learned he refuses every attempt and will rise up against anything or anyone that tries to put him or Jesus Christ (Who he is so passionate about) in their little traditional box.

"He is a 'Word-smith', who has diligently, through hours of investigating God's Word and prayer honed his craft to a fine art; for this reason, his pen (now keyboard) has become a precision tool in the hands of Almighty God.

"He has been given insights into God's Word and a mandate to open the eyes of the believer's understanding, empower The Church to walk in their AUTHORITY and FREEDOM; repair the breach in the walls of TRUTH, and restore PATHS OF RIGHTEOUSNESS to walk in."

Aaron Jones
Revivalist, Author and Artist
September 12, 2017
Sand Springs, Oklahoma

The WISDOM of The JUST

Understanding Iniquity and Carnality

by
Ed Marr

BOLD TRUTH
PUBLISHING

Christian Literature & Artwork
A BOLD TRUTH Publication

The WISDOM of The JUST
Understanding Iniquity and Carnality
Copyright © 2017 Ed Marr

■ FIRST EDITION ■

ISBN 13: 978-0-9991469-7-2

BOLD TRUTH PUBLISHING
(Christian Literature & Artwork)
606 West 41st, Ste. 4
Sand Springs, Oklahoma 74063
www.BoldTruthPublishing.com

Available from Amazon.com and other retail outlets. Orders by U.S. trade bookstores and wholesalers. Email *beirep@yahoo.com*

Quantity sales special discounts are available on quantity purchases by corporations, associations, and others. For details, contact the publisher at the address above.

Cover Art & Design by Aaron Jones.

The conclusions, illustrations, opinions and revelations of the author may not necessarily represent the opinions and beliefs of the publisher.

Printed in the USA.
10 17   10 9 8 7 6 5 4 3 2 1

Permissions

That Which is Known is a
Psalm and a Song to Sing

Whereas, every man is character known,
the Psalm of his life is the song of his throne.
And like the Shulamite who loved the song of the king,
her soul longed for a new song to sing.
The psalms of David made known the true heart of a king,
much like the wisdom of Solomon revealed the conscience of all kings.
Therefore, the character known of a righteous man reflects the character of his psalm,
as a new song that he sings to his king!

Content

Content

Section 5

Epilogue

Conclusion

Table of Figures

Author's Preface

Psalms 40:6 NLT
"You take no delight in sacrifices or offerings. Now that you have made me to listen,
I finally understand you don't require burnt offerings or sin offerings."

As I read this verse, my attention was seized. I thought, Lord you are telling me something here! So I asked the question: *"Just how does God make anyone to listen, so that he might understand?"* Intuitively—I knew the answer...*through our adversities in life!*

For example, it was because of the adversities in my life this book was born: it was October 2006. I was the captain of a Full Gospel Businessmen Chapter in my hometown. After the meeting concluded, I walked out to my Cadillac in the parking lot of the hotel. I had never had any difficulty nor forewarning of anything wrong with this vehicle, mechanically; but as soon as I started the ignition, there was nothing! I checked my battery, my horn, my lights and all was well. So I tried several more times to get the Cadillac started. I ended up leaving the vehicle parked at the curb and there it remained for three full weeks!

So I walked three miles home frustrated as all get out. After I arrived home, it wasn't but a few hours later and the main water line broke under my house! So I quickly turned off the water at the street. Now, I had to obtain water from some other source, so I found an outside faucet from another house: it was for sale so I had no problem filling 32 gallons of water (as a daily/weekly quantity) for our daily use. On top of all this, I had little to no money on hand to cover these repairs. So I took care of the problems short term and walked into my den and closed the door. I collapsed in my chair and leaned over my desk. I simply stated out loud, *"Alright Father, you have my attention; what is it?"* The word INIQUITY came to mind. At the time, I knew absolutely nothing about iniquity or carnality. By this I mean the specific breakdown of either of these two words. Now, I have to admit that my previous writings on repentance in my Freedom Books opened my understanding of carnality some, but I still needed to learn and understand more.

In conclusion, this book is the consequence and outcome of my adversities in my life in the month of October 2006. It's my prayer that you (the reader) will benefit with specific working knowledge so that you might **understand**, because you have **listened**!

Now, for those of you who require a more formal debate, I offer the following. Plainly stated, I am not a formally trained or certified psychologist or psychiatrist. Neither am I a [certified, state recognized] expert or therapist in either medical field. But I am a man to whom God has blessed with an awesome thirst for His divine Word, especially with regards to the investigation of His Book—the Holy Scriptures. Although I claim no professional affiliation; however, I am a retired law enforcement officer, and in this capacity I suppose–I am a professional investigator. Having said this, it's my intention to introduce some insights and revelations from Scripture to people everywhere, but especially to those who are members of the Body of Christ.

This book shall serve to reveal to you specific truths of repentance so far as they pertain towards the principles of mind renewal. I use the term *forensics* because it is *a term used to express the practice or study of formal debate.* Of late, over these recent years, the community at large has been introduced to the science of forensics through such televised programs as CSI (Crime Scene Investigator) CSI-Miami, NCIS, and a host of other programs that cater toward this field of criminal science. Consequently, these programs have tapped the social conscience to such a degree that most everyone understands the import of this expression. Much like the word *philosophy*, which Webster's Dictionary defines as: an expression used to explain or otherwise define a certain branch of knowledge or academic study that is devoted to the systematic examination of basic concepts such as wisdom, truth, existence, reality, causality, and freedom! It is also the theory of logical analysis of the principles underlying conduct, thought, knowledge and a study of human morality, character and behavior in addition to mental health and composure of thought life. Hence, and because of this philosophy anyone may learn or become aware of the nomenclature of any particular thing or subject matter and as it pertains to this work–that subject matter is man's INIQUITY.

The title of this book is, **'The Wisdom of the Just'**, and as such is an oxymoron because it is an expression with contradictory words. I must admit that it was not at all simple to come by. However, as compared to my other extensive works, this particular writing is far simpler to have prepared, simply on the basis of its length. But I must exhort you with this thought. Although it was an easier work task for me, I know the conceptual truths herein shall not be easy for some to receive!

Hebrews 5:11-14 NLT
"There is much more we would like to say about this, but it is difficult to explain, ***especially since you are spiritually dull and don't seem to listen.*** *You have been believers so long now that you ought to be teaching others. Instead,* ***you need someone to teach you again the basic things about God's word.*** *You are like babies who need milk and cannot eat solid food. For someone who lives on milk is still an infant and doesn't know how to do what is right. Solid food is for those who are mature, who*

Author's Preface

through training have the skill to recognize the difference between right and wrong."

1 Corinthians 3:1-3 NLT
*"...when I was with you I couldn't talk to you as I would to spiritual people. I had to talk as though you were infants in the Christian life. I had to feed you with milk, not with solid food, **because you weren't ready for anything stronger. And you still aren't ready, for you are still controlled by your sinful nature.**"*

I include these passages above to mean that I have a lot more revelation to say. But these insights are so far out of the box that it would be difficult for me to share and teach, because many are not ready to receive them.

Author's Preface

Introduction

I begin this thesis on the argument that over the last three decades Almighty God has taken me to an area of spiritual insight that has become all encompassing to me. Ever since my law enforcement days, I have been writing. What began as a simple quiet time of 10-15 minutes per day as a new babe in Christ soon became an all ensuing compulsion of scriptural research that would often last for hours each day! Eventually, the Holy Spirit did direct me to prepare simple word studies; of course, these simple word studies became thematic studies, which soon evolved into character studies, even book studies. In these early years, when my friends in the Lord did stop by to visit me at home and they would find me immersed in my writing! So often, they asked me why I was writing so much and my only response to their question was—I just didn't know! What I did know was that I was being compelled to write and that without any understanding as to why.

Even way back then, the Holy Spirit led me into an area of thought pertaining to the renewing of the mind. In fact, I still possess all of my writings to this day and occasionally I glance back at them just to refresh my mind with these profound thoughts. This passion of mine I know is God inspired and is a direct indicator of the gift and calling He has deposited within me as an ingredient of His character. And throughout the years, this passion has not let up; for I have felt and borne the weight of its pressure continuously, (much like a scuba diver would experience the weight and the pressure of deep water). What's more, just as the scuba diver inhales the pressurized air mix in his scuba tank, I too have inhaled the pressurized air stream of God through the regulator called; the Holy Spirit!

Now the word *nomenclature* is defined as a systematic means to assign names to objects, items or organisms in a particular science, art, or scientific classification system (Taxonomy). Hence, this *taxonomy* is the practice or principles of classification. (Webster's) As you read this work, you will be introduced to the spiritual nomenclature of iniquity as the basis for your carnality. In fact, carnality may be considered as a shell in which iniquity is contained.

As a case in point, in the summer of 1971 I was stationed in Saigon as a Marine Security Guard. One day the starboard side of the Marine Guard Detachment spent the day at a military beach community in the South China Sea for a bit of R & R. Having spent the entire day at the beach, it came time for the company muster prior to departing back to Saigon and our barracks. The Lieutenant conducted the muster (roll call) and we all responded as our individual names were called out. Corporal R. P. however, never did respond to his name; it was obvious to all that he had left the area. So after searching for him in the immediate area and not locating him on land, the lieutenant had the presence of mind to look for him out at sea. He spotted a little black dot adrift in the water estimated to be some 2 miles out. Suddenly, I hear my name, Sergeant Marr front and center! Right then my suspicion was confirmed, for I intuitively knew that Corporal R.P. had most likely drifted out to sea and probably due to his drunkenness. I presented myself to the lieutenant. He ordered me to retrieve R.P. The Lieutenant handed me his binoculars and I looked in the direction indicated for R.P. He was a little speck out there in the deep blue alright! I too estimated him to be about 2 miles out.

Since I was the best swimmer present, I donned my snorkeling gear and proceeded towards R.P. While I made my way out to sea, the farther I swam, the deeper and darker the water became. During my rescue operation, I saw several large shadows and other dark shapes cruising by beneath me. These things certainly caused me to be concerned for my safety. At one point, I nearly swam into a large jellyfish that appeared in front of me at the surface! Well, I eventually did catch R.P. who was as red as a lobster and who had passed out on a large inner tube. I secured my web belt to his belt and towed the tube with this drunk on it back to shore.

Although this event was an experience I had back in the day, I only mention it to make the following point. As pertaining to the Word of God, there are levels and depths Almighty God would have all His children to go. However, in spite of His desire for us, most people prefer to remain at the surface or near the shore. They fail to realize that it is out in the deep where God's mighty works are encountered!

> *Psalms 107:23-24 AMP*
> *"Some go down to the sea and travel over it in ships to do business in great waters; these see the works of the Lord and His wonders in the deep."*

> *Psalms 90:8 AMP*
> *"Our iniquities, our secret heart and its sins [which we would so like to conceal even from ourselves], You have set in the [revealing] light of Your countenance."*

Now, nautically speaking, every six feet of depth is equivalent to a fathom. Applying this to Scripture, there are fathoms in God very few dare to come to know. It is only in these depths of God where His wonders are seen. His wonders in the deep also apply towards the depths of your soul where iniquity resides! Those shadows and dark shapes that I observed cruise by beneath me way back then are representative of those things lurking within the depths of my soul which do in fact scare me or at the very least present a cause for concern. Occasionally, these dark shadows and shapes do come to the surface in life like a large breaching whale and when they do, turbulence at the surface occurs. Perhaps you can relate to this for yourself?

As another case in point, have you ever considered the volcano? Why do they exist and to what purpose do they provide or serve? Sometime ago while reading about volcanoes, the following reality came to mind. Planet earth has many volcanoes and just as each volcano has the many subterranean lava tubes through which flows of magma travel to the surface and just as each volcano has its own magma boiling in a cauldron waiting to explode into the atmosphere, so likewise does every human being possess similar traits within their soul! These physical volcanoes represent that which lies deep within each of us. And just as volcanoes erupt, so likewise do we erupt whenever our life situation triggers our suppressed emotional magma!

The following work is my humble attempt to share with you the wonders of God that I have observed for myself. I share this with you in hopes that you would be encouraged to go down to the sea yourself and know that there is nothing to fear but your own stuff! But know this, Almighty God is there waiting for you for He dwells in the deep, and it is His truth that he desires to be deep in you! He is our Heavenly Father who beckons one and all to launch out into the deep, as though you were embarking upon a search and rescue mission with Him to save yourself from those dark shapes and shadows that cruise by within the depths of your soul.

Psalms 139: 1-16 THE MESSAGE
"God, investigate my life, get all the facts firsthand. I'm an open book to you; even from a distance, you know what I am thinking. You know when I leave and when I get back; I'm never out of your sight. You know everything I'm going to say before I start the first sentence. I look behind me and you're there, then up ahead and you're there, too—your reassuring presence, coming and going. This is too much, too wonderful—I can't take it all in!"

"Is there any place I can go to avoid your Spirit; to be out of your sight? If I climb to the sky, you're there! If I go underground, you're there! If I flew on morning's wings to the far western horizon, you would find me in a minute—you're already there waiting! Then I said to myself, Oh, he even sees me in the dark! At night AI

am immersed in the Light! It's a fact: darkness isn't dark to you; night and day, darkness and light, they're all the same to you. Oh yes, you shaped me first inside, then out; you formed me in my mother's womb, I thank you, High God—you're breathtaking! Body and soul, I am marvelously made! I worship in adoration— what a creation! You know me inside and out, you know every bone in my body; you know exactly how I was made, bit-by-bit, how I was sculpted from nothing into something. Like an open book, you watched me grow from conception to birth; all the stages of my life were spread out before you, the days of my life all prepared before I'd ever lived one day."

"Blessings are upon the head of the [uncompromisingly] righteous (the upright, in right standing with God)…The memory of the [uncompromisingly] righteous is a blessing… The wise in heart will accept and obey commandments…He who walks uprightly walks securely…but he who boldly reproves makes peace…the mouth of the [uncompromising- ly] righteous man is a well of life…On the lips of him who has discernment skillful and Godly wisdom is found…Wise men store up knowledge [in mind and heart]…"
Proverbs 10:6-14 AMP

"And he shall go before him in the spirit and power of Ē-lias,
to turn the hearts of the fathers to the children,
and the disobedient to **the WISDOM of the JUST***;*
to make ready a people prepared for the Lord."
Luke 1:17

Section 1

➜ The Alpha and the Omega ⬅

The way I see it, the problem is people traditionally prefer God to be one thing and not the other! With man's religions we make God to be high but never low; we make Him the one thing and not the other so far as it strokes our creature comforts, but we choose to deny Him as the other. This one sided view of God only impedes our spiritual development in that we shall never come to know Who God is and what we are as long as we prefer to discount all that God is, even if it challenges our present theologies. In order for any man to come to that place of knowing, he first must acquire key principles of understanding and knowledge, for as *Hosea 4:1-6* states, *My people perish for lack of knowledge [of God]*. In other words, we don't perish for lack of the knowledge of the Devil or Satan, although our religions would say otherwise!

Revelations 1:8 KJV
"I AM the Alpha and Omega, the beginning and the end."

Revelations 22:13 DRA
"I AM Alpha and Omega, the first and the last..."

Revelations 1:17-18 KJV
"Fear not; I AM the first and the last: I AM He that liveth, and was dead, and, behold. I AM alive forevermore, Amen; and have the keys of hell and of death."

2 Samuel 24:1 KJV
"And the anger of the Lord was kindled against Israel, and He moved David against them to say, Go, number Israel and Judah!"

1 Chronicles 21:1 KJV
"And Satan stood up against Israel and provoked David to number Israel."

What is Scripture saying here? Could it be that Scripture contradicts itself? Or could it be that our misinterpretation and transliteration of Scripture are the real issue? Just look at the last two verses. Is Scripture informing us that there are two sides or aspects to God? By explanation, *Alpha and Omega means there is a polarity with and about Almighty God and He is everything and all things in between!*

He is the right from the left and the left from the right! He is the sum and the substance; He is the Light and the Darkness, Who created the Light! He is the First and the Last as well as the End from the Beginning! He is the Question and the Answer!

Almighty God is the Here and the There; He is the NOW as well as the PAST! He is No Where and He is Now Here! He is the Bitter and the Sweet as well as the Alphabet (in any language) from A to Z! He is every letter of every word ever spoken or written, and in this context He is the Profound, the Provocative and the Profane; He is the Lord God Almighty! [But is He really Satan?] After all, He has created evil and the darkness of man's iniquity; is that just a part of Him which is (less than) Himself as contrasted to (or a diversity of) His Magnificent God Self (LIGHT)?

⚷

In order for any man to come to that place of knowing, he first must acquire key principles of understanding and knowledge,

And what's more, He holds the keys, (principle knowledge) of hell and of death! It is therefore reasonable to state that Almighty God desires that humanity acquire this carnal knowledge on this side of the grave so far as, this knowledge pertains to our INIQUITY (Lie - Based Thinking).

Again I repeat *Psalms 40:6 "You take no delight in sacrifices or offerings. Now that **you have made me to listen, I finally understand** you don't require burnt offerings or sin offerings."*

So join me now as we unlock the mysteries using the keys of this specific knowledge which mandates **our personal involvement, our inner commitments and our emotional attachments**, because these three virtues fully describe for us the definition of the *"Da'ath Elohim"* (the Knowledge of God).

The following insights will hopefully help you to learn and understand the concept of our make up, physically and spiritually. These insights are my feeble attempt to express the *forensic breakdown* of our carnal flesh and self.

→ The King of Terrors ←

On Sunday, January 6th, 2008 while taking a shower with soapsuds in my hair, the following was spoken to me: *"The fear of death is exploited because death is man's greatest fear!"* I immediately thought there was something in the soapsuds or the water! But as I thought on this a while and then, sharing this spiritual concept with my son (Ed), my mind considered just how often and how much man's fear of death is used by all facets of society.

For example, insurance companies exploit fear to reap their profits from the masses. Politicians use fear tactics to persuade the citizens of America for one agenda or another, even their own! Also, within the corporate world fear is used as a ruse to convince people to purchase their products or services, even when there is no obvious need. So also in any relationship, one spouse or significant other may use fear tactics as a means of control or manipulation.

And finally, even in the religious circle, fear is exploited to maintain a fear based theology sustaining a religious hierarchy! *In other words, Lie - Based Religion is the foundation of a any Fear Based Theology; just as any Lie - Based Societal rule is the foundation for our fear ridden societies!*

All of this is done to benefit the few at the expense of the (ignorant and cowardly) masses. In effect, the exploitation of fear is nothing more than taking selfish or unfair advantage of a person or situation all for personal gain!

> *Job 18:14 AMP*
> *"He shall be rooted out of his dwelling place in which he trusted, and he shall be brought to the king of terrors (death)."*

> *Luke 18:1 AMP*
> *"Also Jesus told them a parable to the effect that they ought always to pray **and not to turn coward** (faint, lose heart and give up)"*

It takes courage to confront our stuff, doesn't it? Scripture implies that the fear of death is *a king of terror,* even above all other phobias that we have! This means that no matter what other fear of terror a man might possess, is only subservient to the King of all Terrors [DEATH]. And speaking of kings, *it takes a king to overpower another king!*

Doesn't Scripture state that all believers have already been made kings and priests unto God? *(cf: Re 1:6 and 5:10)*

Here in the following Scripture passages we learn that:
Death is a gift? *(cf: 1 Co 3:21-22)*
That death is the last enemy that shall be destroyed! *(cf: 1 Co 15:26)*

1 Corinthians 15:55 even asks the question... *O death, where is thy sting O grave, where is they victory?"* This means that individually, each one of us may overcome this king of terror within our own life!

So what are your fears? Let's see, there are many fears: fear of success, fear of heights, fear of failure, fear of rejection, fear of commitment, fear of man, fear of public speaking, fear of spiders, fear of love, and the list goes on; doesn't it? Since we all believe in that which we feel, then these feelings must have their root in some other thing or source that has implanted or embedded itself within the framework of our mind. The other thing must be our iniquitous thought life (what I call *Lie - Based Thinking*)!

Now, I believe people fear what they don't understand as well as that which may be different from themselves, their institutions and their traditions. It is also commonly known that acquired knowledge dispels fear. *Hosea 4:6* states, *"My people perish for lack of knowledge, but you have rejected knowledge..."* Notice here, that Scripture does not say that people perish because of Satan! We perish because of our fear and willful ignorance! OUCH!!!!

Scripture also states in *Romans 8*, *"For to be carnally minded is death, but to be spiritually minded is life and peace."* So this carnal mindedness must pertain also to ignorance; and this ignorance must be the same as death, in our emotional, physical and spiritual realm.

But what does religion really know about death? It seems to me that religious institutions should serve humanity to overcome their fear of death and do so by providing specific knowledge of love and courage. But wait a minute! All you need is faith they say, and faith works by love. But my question is, does merely reciting the word *faith* over come this king of terror or is it the application of love that will overcome this terror?

Since Scripture does state that *"perfect love casts out fear and he that feareth is not perfected in love."* I like how the Amplified states it, *1 John 4:18 "there is no fear in love [dread does* *not exist], but full grown (complete, perfect) love turns fear out of doors and **expels every trace of terror!** For fear brings with it the thought of punishment and [so] he who is afraid has not reached full maturity of love [is not yet grown into love's complete perfection]."*

It seems to me that when the institutionalized church finally embraces repentance as *God's Divine Remedy for man's carnal tragedy,* the masses will be able to eliminate their iniquitous thoughts, or at the very least—be aware of there existence. Once our iniquitous thoughts have been eradicated (or captured and brought into the obedience of Christ), then the perceived separation would also vanish; for it never existed anyway. *In other words, any (concocted) religious separation between God and man was/is merely an imagined reality via a crafty ruse to sway the masses.*

8—

This means that individually, each one of us may overcome this king of terror within our own life!

Isaiah 59:2 KJV
*"But **your iniquities have separated you** from your God and your sin (transgressions that stem from iniquitous thoughts) has turned His face from you that He cannot hear,"*

Ephesians 2:14 KJV
*"For He is our peace, who hath made both one, and hath **broken down the middle wall of partition** (separation) between us, "*

➔ Breaking Down the Fourth Wall ⬅

Notice the phrase, *broken down the middle wall,* in *Ephesians 2:14* above. What is this wall? Is it possible to describe this wall? And once it is described, is it actually possible to recognize the wall within our own iniquitous thoughts, that is, our carnal mind? So let's see what happens, okay?

There are physical walls and there are invisible (conscious and subconscious) walls. Obviously, any physical wall is a partition separating us from another environment or atmosphere, right? In similar manner of construct, the invisible wall(s) are also built.

The WISDOM of The JUST

For example, in the entertainment industry, they have an expression called, *breaking down the fourth wall*; every director, producer, stagehand, actor and prop maker knows this principle to be the key that embraces the audience. This perceived barrier (wall) exists between a theatrical stage, the movie screen, television or the computer and the audience or individual watching at home. *(See Fig. 1)*

(Figure 1)

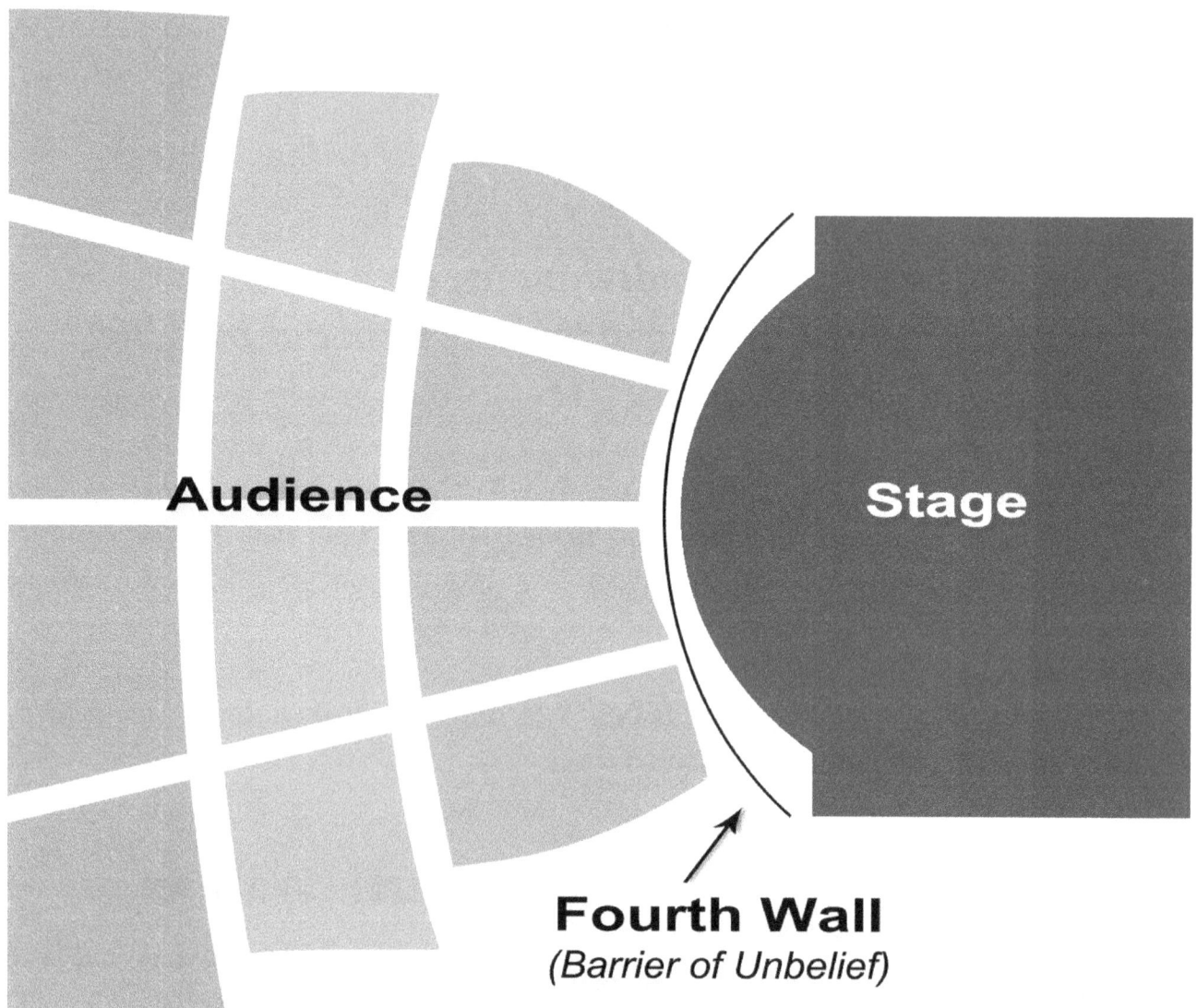

Audience

Stage

Fourth Wall
(Barrier of Unbelief)

It is this barrier of imagination through which people are able to tap into the make believe, if even for a few minutes a day or for hours at a time; in fact, virtual reality has the power to convince a person of a particular fantasy or notion and compel his interaction. We see this with sophisticated equipment such as flight, combat and police simulators in which these personnel train in a controlled virtual environment.

In fact, just a few years ago, I saw a anti-smoking commercial on the television which illustrated this concept of a wall very dramatically. In the commercial, a persons face and head are seen, as the voice over spoke, the head and face rotated around; soon there appeared a theatrical stage on the back half of the person's skull, with a wall separating the seemingly conscience from the subconscience.

But getting back to my topic specifically, the spirit of the mind is said to have a theater as well and in like fashion, the mind can play out imaginative scenarios that are mentally perceived—since all of us think in pictures. In this capacity individually, each person is their own main character; and all locations where a person might roam, experience or reside becomes the back drop for an on going drama!

Notes:_____

_____

_____

_____

_____

_____

_____

_____

_____

_____

_____

The WISDOM of The JUST

Notes:_____

_____

_____

_____

_____

_____

_____

_____

_____

_____

_____

_____

_____

_____

_____

_____

_____

_____

_____

_____

Section 2

→ Humus and the Dirt of Humanity ←

I asked God this question, *"Why is the human race called humanity, human beings or human?"* So I did some research, and this is what I found. *Humus* is defined as *that which comes from dirt!* Gold, diamonds, and all precious stones are extracted from the dirt. Oil and coal are tow (drag) resources which are excavated from the dirt. When we die, guess what? Our bodies decompose and return to dirt (dust of the ground). I've read that there are 78 elements of dirt found in the human body and that these elements are also found in the oceans, as well as, in the theater of the celestial!

Genesis 2:7 NLT (brackets mine)
"Then the Lord God formed the man from the dust of the ground. He breathed the breath of life into the man's nostrils, and the man became a living [soul] person."

The definition above denotes that HUMUS consists of animal excrement. Isn't that just wonderful to know? *To think that dung beetles might live in me! Yuk!* Be that as it may, just as there are bodily droppings left behind by one and all, so too are spiritual deposits left behind within the soul of every man, ever born! These deposits are like spiritual land mines (iniquity) the demonic have dropped across the vast landscape of a person's soul; much like a herd of livestock would leave behind in an open field (cow patties). Similarly, like any dog kennel in need of being cleaned up. No wonder Paul said of himself, *Oh wretched man that I am who shall deliver me from the body of this death? (cf. Ro 7:24)*

Applying these land mines towards man's cluttered soul, it is apparent we all have a cleanup job to do. And by this I mean too say, that the multitude of our iniquities has accumulated for so long, all because of our neglect to keep ourselves spotless (without blemish or free of any unclean thing), and because of this neglect; we are not much different than a sack of steer fertilizer. *(cf: 2 Ti 2:19-21)*

→ The Nomenclature of Our Spiritual DNA ←

Biologically and forensically it has been shown that all things have a spiral genetic code [genetic information] known as a double helix. Within this helix are found microscopic molecules (chromosomes). Altogether these chromosomes form a multicolored ladder that contain or consist of rungs upon which DNA is either formed or found. DNA is the acronym for *(deoxyribonucleic acid)*. Since this is a physiological reality and is an excellent means of personal identification and description in the natural, so likewise there is a spiritual DNA (Divine Nature of the Almighty) that God has predesigned and deliberately consigned and or conscripted as a spiritual equivalent! You could say this DNA is *His fingerprint* upon His creation as well as *His signature*! Not only did He create all that exists, but also He autographed it Himself!

Notice the first three letters of the bio-technical name of DNA, *DEO*. According to Webster's, *Deo* is said *to imply or mean a recognition that is given or attributed to Creator God!* So then, by its very name, scientifically speaking, it is [a given] as a presupposition that DNA has its origin (source, starting point) in and from Almighty God! And just as all gifts and callings in man are His, upon our passing these shall return to Him from whence they came! This is also true of DNA!

Jeremiah 1:4-5 AMP
"Then the word of the Lord came to me [Jeremiah] saying, before I formed you in the womb I knew [and] approved of you [as My chosen instrument], and before you were born I separated and set you apart, consecrating you: [and] I appointed you [as a prophet to the nations]."

Isaiah 49:1-8 AMP
"Listen to me, O isles and coastlands, and hearken, you people from afar. The Lord has called me from the womb; from the body of my mother He has named my name. And He has made my mouth like a sharp sword; in the shadow of His hand has He hid me and made me a polished arrow; in His quiver has He kept me close and concealed me. And the Lord said to me, you are my servant, Israel [you who strive with God and with men and prevail], in whom I will be glorified…yet surely my right hand is with the Lord, and my recompense is with my God. And now, says the Lord—who formed me from the womb to be His servant to bring Jacob back to Him and that Israel might be gathered to Him and not be swept away, for I am honorable in the eyes of the Lord and my God has become my strength…"

Isaiah 41:15-16 NKJV
"Behold, I will make you to be a new sharp threshing instrument which has teeth;

you shall thresh the mountains and beat them small, and shall make the hills like chaff. You shall winnow them, and the wind shall carry them away, and the tempest or whirlwind shall scatter them. And you shall rejoice in the Lord, you shall glory in the Holy One of Israel." (cf. Isa 54:15-17)

These passages and so many more describe or define and even provide a nomenclature of spiritual DNA! And to properly apprehend the significance of a spiritual nomenclature I must establish a foundation of interpretation of meaning. By *nomenclature*, I mean too say *the descriptive breakdown of component parts or elements that work in concert with all other parts or elements of my spiritual constitution, which in their cohesive codependence of each other altogether comprise of the man and servant—who is Ed Marr.*

⛁⚊

You could say this DNA is His fingerprint upon His creation as well as His signature! Not only did He create all that exists, but also He autographed it Himself!

I invite you to take a look at pages 18-24 on water droplets. You will discover through (commentary and photographs) how positive and negative sounds shape water droplets at the molecular level. Together, this section coincides with man's spiritual DNA because of the influence of Godliness or of man's iniquity (lie - based thinking). And when you consider that every man is approximately 70% water; coupled with, we inhabit a planet that is ¾ covered by water, it is no coincidence or wonder this occurs. What's more, is the scriptural truth that there does exist a washing of the Word of Regeneration, and as you look at these photographs of water crystals keep in mind how they have been regenerated through the spoken Word! (cf. *Tit 3:5*) Awesome!!!!

➔ The Theory of Intelligent Design ⬅

It was the fall season of 2007 when I was positioned at the ORU's north Gate birddogging the Robert's Mansion. I was thinking of the notion of what is the spirit of the Mind? I mean, what makes it such? I thought of the concept of intelligent design and specifically of *Psalms 139:14* which states that *I am fearfully and wonderfully made.*

It is common knowledge that at every level of creation, design or development *intelli-*

gent design must be evident. For example, a beautiful Cadillac evinces *intelligent design* at each and every level of assembly; from the thought of the designer, to his blueprints, to the fabrication of the smallest component and throughout the assembly process, until finally with all parts put together intelligently, you have this beautiful vehicle.

Likewise, the computer is able to do all it does because of the fabrication of the smallest and perhaps least significant element to the most important parts; all combined together allow the computer to function as it does, (intelligently,) and all because of intelligent design at each level of assembly.

With this in mind, I realized the spirit of my mind consists of the evidence of intelligent design as found in the cellular, even down to the molecular content of my DNA. This infers that biologists have discovered that intelligent design is found within the very molecules of our anatomy! And when I consider there are literally trillions of molecules that make up a person's physical anatomy, the combined affect of this intelligent design comprises what is known as the spirit of the mind which (envelopes, saturates and permeates our entire body! So then, the spirit of the mind does not exist in the head only but it exists in and throughout my entire physical anatomy!)

> *Psalms 139:13-16 THE MESSAGE*
> *"Oh yes, you shaped me first inside, then out; you formed me in my mother's womb. I thank you, High God—you're breathtaking! Body and Soul, I am marvelously made! I worship in adoration—what a creation!* **You know me inside and out, you know every bone in my body; you know exactly how I was made, bit by bit how I was sculpted from nothing into something.** *Like an open book, you watched me grow from conception to birth; all the stages of my life were spread out before you, the days of my life all prepared before I'd even lived one day."*

In other words, the mind is not only located and or restricted to one's head, as I once thought, but it is found in and throughout our anatomy! So then, with this in mind, since we read in Scripture that we are to renew the spirit of our mind, it must appertain towards every molecule that contains (and is the essence of) intelligent design anatomically! Hence, when a person renews his or her mind, the process of renewal is the causative effect of physical, mental and emotional healings and cures; because a renewed mind eliminates Lie - Based Thinking (Iniquity).

The outcome of which will be speedily realized at that particular level of development.

This then provides some insight to *Ephesians 4:15-17*. Paul concludes his analogy in *verse 17* by speaking of the vanity of the mind. He prefaces this with the concept of intelligent design (that Creator God had revealed to him), that exists in all things created in the Body of Christ.

Regarding Iniquity, since iniquity resides within the spirit of the mind, which I define or describe to be the cohesive and coalesced result of intelligent design, it stands too reason that iniquity is also found within and at the molecular level even pathogenically! [Remember the volcano.] Furthermore, since the mind is a spirit, it is comparable to the soul and this means that my body is not a container for my soul but that my soul envelops my entire physical being! WOW!!!!!!!!

And whereas Creator God breathed the breath of life into man, His breath is that which originates from the very soul/Spirit of God Himself! In other words, just as there is no end or beginning to the air we all breathe, so also there is no end or beginning with God's Spirit/Soul! And just as the air in one room may differ from another in aroma, so likewise there are varying atmospheres within God's soul. These different atmospheres (ethers) then are experienced in that miniaturized soul of God found essentially imbued as that which has been saturated with something divine as with a substance, upon and within all of creation!

This then means that all things created consist in and because of the Spirit of God. This also means that the Spirit of God in me makes me God Himself albeit, miniaturized! And just as my DNA numbers into the trillions so likewise that I AM a molecule of God as is each and every other person as well as all things created in His ever-expanding universe! No wonder Scripture says that there is none else; I know not any!

Isaiah 45:6 AMP
"That men may know from the east and the rising of the sun and from the west and the setting of the sun that there is no [other] God besides ME. I AM the Lord, and none else [is He]."

The WISDOM of The JUST

Notes:_____

_____

_____

_____

_____

_____

_____

_____

_____

_____

_____

_____

_____

_____

_____

_____

_____

_____

_____

_____

_____

→ Did Jesus Have Iniquity? ←

While en route to work one day, I demanded that God speak to me. I suppose the challenges that my immediate family had faced over those recent weeks were catching up to me. On 12-24-07 my sister-in-law Louise's dad passed away. Then on 12-30-07 my nephew John David was killed in a hunting incident. In addition, my younger brother Rick was in the ICU ward of the VA Hospital in Baltimore, Maryland and was recovering from spinal cord surgery, which took place on January 4, 2008. So to counteract this despair, I really needed something other than these events to contemplate.

So while on routine patrol, I pondered the notion of God's Magnificence and His Less than Magnificent God-Self. Specifically as these aspects of His nature towards His Goodness and Mercy contrasted with iniquity and evil, which as Scriptures states He created. *(cf. Isa 45:7)* The following is my thought process…

Isaiah 59:2 KJV
"But your iniquities have separated you from your God and your sin has turned His face from you that He cannot hear."

2 Corinthians 5:21 KJV
"He who knew no sin became sin for us that we might be made the righteousness of God through Him."

Although Jesus Christ knew no sin, *does not imply that He possessed no iniquity!* This is a very bold statement I know and it took me several weeks to consider. As Isaiah above indicates, iniquity and sin are 2 different things. Where iniquity pertains toward the premeditations of the spirit of the mind (heart, aka Lie-Based Thinking), sin is the acting out of these disingenuous deceptions and become our transgressions.

So this thought came to mind, that perhaps Jesus Christ did have iniquitous thoughts just as any other man, for how could He become His Magnificent God-Self and Savior of the world as the Son of God without that side of His God-Self that was less than magnificent?

2 Corinthians 10:3-6 AMPC
"For though we walk (live) in the flesh, we are not carrying on our warfare to the flesh and using more human weapons. For the weapons of our warfare are

not physical [weapons of flesh and blood], but they are mighty before God for the overthrow and destruction of strongholds. [In as much as we] refute arguments, theories and reasoning's and the ever proud and lofty thing that sets itself up against the knowledge of God; and we lead every thought and purpose away captive into obedience of Christ (the Messiah, the Anointed One), being in readiness to punish every [insubordinate for his] disobedience, [as a church] are fully secured and complete."

8—

Every man ever born was also created in the image and likeness of God, spiritually just as you are and I AM created in the image and likeness of God, spiritually.

Hebrews 4:14-16 NLT
"So then, since we have a great High Priest who has entered heaven, Jesus the Son of God, let us hold firmly to what we believe. This High Priest of ours UNDERSTANDS our weaknesses (Iniquities), for He faced all of the same testing's (temptations) we do, yet He did not sin. So let us come boldly to the throne of our gracious God. There we will receive His mercy, and we will find grace when we need it most."

Hebrews 5:8 KJV
"Though he was a son, yet he learned his obedience by the things which he suffered."

My first question is, how could Jesus be tempted without iniquity? If He did not have iniquitous thoughts then He would have an unfair advantage over the rest of us, don't you think? These verses provide a powerful clue into this notion that Jesus did in fact have to deal with iniquity! Although He struggled with his iniquity, these Scriptures state— HE KNEW NO SIN! For me, this implies that Jesus Christ controlled His thoughts; thereby, capturing His Lie - Based Thinking (as that part of His Less than magnificent God Self) and that He came to demonstrate for each of us [how] that we can do the same! *(cf. Jo 5:24)* This is why I think Jesus understands our weakness!

Now Jesus Christ was born of a Virgin. Although He had every opportunity to sin—He chose not to, ever! So where did His iniquity come from? Jesus Christ was/is God and yet, born a man; His iniquity had to originate from someone or from some place other than Satan. I propose to you that God created the iniquity that Jesus Christ did have as that which represents (His Less than Magnificent God-Self). In other words, Satan did not have anything to do with it! WOW!!!

This Spiritual Concept provides powerful insight into the mystery of our own iniquities, does it not? Namely, that since all of humanity was (is) created in the image and likeness of God Who is Spirit, this has to mean that our iniquity also came from God and it is to Him we all must come with our questions to get the answers even though we may or may not care to hear. Consider the following Scriptures that support the claim: God created evil and our iniquity.

Isaiah 45:6-7 AMPC
"That men may know from the east and the rising of the sun and from the west and the setting of the sun that there is no God besides Me. I AM the Lord, and no one else [is He]. I form the light and create darkness, I make peace and I create [physical] evil (calamity); I AM the Lord who does all these things."

Ecclesiastes 3:10a, 11b KJV
"I have seen the travail, which God hath given to the sons of men to be exercised in it… so that no man can find out the work that God maketh from the beginning to the end."

Ecclesiastes 7:13-14 KJV
"Consider the work of God: for who can make straight which He hath made crooked? In the day of prosperity be joyful, but in the day of adversity consider: God also hath set the one over against the other, to the end that man should find nothing after him."

Job 42:10a, 11b KJV
"And the Lord turned the captivity of Job…and comforted him over all the evil that the Lord had brought upon him…"

Now Jesus Christ is the expressed image and likeness of God spiritually. Every man ever born was also created in the image and likeness of God, spiritually just as you are and I AM created in the image and likeness of God, spiritually. We were never created in the image and likeness of Satan! My point is this: My magnificent Ed self cannot exist without that which is less than magnificent existing within me, *for I AM what I am not! For how could I ever hope to be who and what I am now unless I had that which I am not within me?* My magnificent Ed Self and my less than magnificent Ed Self are both created by God and it seems that Satan had nothing to do with it!

What then can be said of this Satan? *Could it be that Satan is a concoction of religious hyperbole (exaggeration, overstatement)? Could it be that religious institutions perpetuate this mythology for their own existence at the expense of the masses? Could it be that the Scriptures themselves are tainted with a particular bias in this regard? (See p. 97)* Is it possible that the very Bible itself has been mistranslated by oppressed scribes at the behest of the powers that be of their day and time? In other words, *anything that man touches is found to be tampered with and that either directly or circumstantially!*

In conclusion then, the above observations point me in a fresh new direction regarding all the traditional church has taught about sin that separates, condemnation, eternal hell fire, etc. I cannot be afraid to follow where this knowledge takes me, and neither should you!

→ Water Droplets ←

It is very important that we fully comprehend just what occurs as we speak and how it affects us, and to what degree our negative thoughts and words impact, infect and damage our physical bodies with disease; not to mention, the world around us and within us. Aside from the *spirit of Error* we verbally insert within ourselves—our daily conversation (either positive or negative) changes or [creates] our world. The following (Water Drops) are photographs taken from the website of Dr. Marusa Emoto and are used by permission.] *(See photos - Figs. 2-5, p. 22-23)*

> *Proverbs 18:21 AMP*
> *"Death and life are in the power of the tongue, and they who indulge in it shall eat the fruit of it [for death or life]."*

God knows what He is doing: God's judgments are redemptive

> *Isaiah 26:9 KJV*
> *With my soul have I desired thee in the night; yea, with my spirit within me will I seek thee early: for when thy judgments are in the earth, the inhabitants of the world will learn righteousness.*

All of the calamities in the earth today are just birth pangs heralding a new world to come.

In the mean time we must fulfill what God has called us to do in the time we have left.

It was June 5th 2013. I was attending the Wednesday evening service at my church. While inside and during the Praise and Worship service, I suddenly experienced a complete numbness and tingling sensation overcome my physical body. I began to collapse to the floor in the darkened auditorium. I caught myself and staggered out the rear doors into the main lobby. I stumbled over to the coffee bar where I met several others. I poured myself a cup of coffee. I reached for it with my left hand. I turned towards the folks there and spilled my coffee onto the floor! In fact, I dropped the cup! The people said that I didn't look to well. I sat down and rested, trying to regain my composure. The numbness and tingling sensations never left. So I went home and slept it off. As I awoke Thursday morning, I noticed that the numbness and the tingling were still with me. It was at this time that I sought medical help. I walked over to the emergency care clinic and as soon as I stepped up to the office check in window, the nurse called for help from the staff there at the clinic. The ambulance was called and I was taken to the hospital for a possible stroke!

After I was released from the hospital, I was taken home where I recovered from this ordeal. Now I just had open-heart surgery in March of 2011 from which I expired. I was informed that I had checked out and was gone for 28 minutes!

I sat in my apartment alone crying out to God for an explanation, as I knew in my heart that He had other purposes for me. So he teaches me the following:

As I sat there in my easy chair, the Holy Spirit said the following. *Tenderness and love will always conquer violence and hate!* He explained this statement via the plants and sound waves. In essence, the Holy Spirit taught me that when I speak softly and tenderly to my situations in my life, the frequency of sound does resonate within and into the physical object such as a house plant or other object, even my own body. So he told me to speak healthful words to my physical organ, my heart. But I objected because I have always invoked the healing Scriptures over my entire body, loudly with much gusto! I mean, that's just the way I have always seen it done!

But when I realized the error of this abrupt or forceful technique, I immediately felt a warm tingling sensation occur within my chest! So I took the initiative and prayed over every organ in my body. I was amazed to feel my body absorbing the prayers of thankfulness and love. WOW!!! What an experience that was then and still is today!

I compared this to a law enforcement officer commanding a suspect to comply with forceful and overbearing words. I also thought of the violent and hateful lyrics of some songs accompanied by the heavy rock music. All this too say, that this experience helped me to appreciate, know and understanding the principle of love. Why, because love overcomes hate, light overcomes darkness, and demons are defeated when they run into God-like qualities in the saints of God. As Christians we either empower Love or we empower the hate and violence around about us. It may come to you as a shock that *all of us Christians in our daily lives empower the destructive forces around us.* We are told that we must not give place to the devil. *(e.g., Ephesians 4:26-27)* and that *Death and Life are in the power of the tongue. (cf. Pr 18:21)*

Adversity feeds off what we speak and what we emanate: Harsh words emanate a power, which stands in opposition. When you speak harshly to your children you weaken their dignity. Negative, destructive words towards one's spouse feeds the evil powers around them. Words are power, especially when they come from the mouths of spirit-filled Christians. *The Sermon on the Mount* is a masterpiece of divine strategy for defeating the enemy. Because we are made in the image of God and God creates through the Words He speaks, our words also have enormous power. Does the Word not say that *we are gods;*

Psalms 82:6 KJV
I have said, Ye are gods; and all of you are children of the most High.

John 10:34-35 KJV
Jesus answered them, "Is it not written in your law, I said, Ye are gods? If he called them gods, unto whom the word of God came, and the scripture cannot be broken;"

This is why the Bible says the tongue can be set on fire from Hell and is a very dangerous part of our anatomy, and can be used for great good or great evil.

Proverbs 21:23 KJV
Whoso keepeth his mouth and his tongue keepeth his soul from troubles.

James 3:5-6, 10 KJV
5 Even so the tongue is a little member, and boasteth great things. Behold, how great a matter a little fire kindleth!
6 And the tongue is a fire, a world of iniquity: so is the tongue among our members, that it defileth the whole body, and setteth on fire the course of nature; and it is set

on fire of hell.
10 Out of the same mouth proceedeth blessing and cursing. My brethren, these things ought not so to be.

It is all a matter of who you are empowering: If we don't learn to guard our mouth, the coming darkness will overpower us. A friend alerted me to a book by a Dr Masaru Emoto called "The Hidden Messages in Water"

Until the ground breaking work of this pioneer Japanese researcher whose astonishing discovery about water, documented photographically, changed most of what we didn't know and led to a new consciousness of Earth's most precious resource.

Dr. Masaru Emoto was born in Japan and is a graduate of the Yokohama Municipal University and the Open International University as a Doctor of Alternative Medicine. His photographs were first featured in his self-published books *Messages from Water 1 and 2*. *The Hidden Messages in Water* was first published in Japan, with over 400,000 copies sold internationally.

⚷

As Christians we either empower love or we empower the hate and violence around about us.

What has put Dr. Emoto at the forefront of the study of water is his proof that our thoughts and feelings effect physical reality. By producing different focused intentions through written and spoken words and music and literally presenting it to the same water samples, the water "changed its expression".

When music from Mozart Symphony was played the Crystals form into the image.

This is very interesting and shows that the life in these crystals responded to music and words. When we realize all things are held together by the life and power of Jesus we see how that life responds to Love, and positive affirmation. *(See photos - Fig. 2. p. 22)*

Colossians 1:16-17 KJV
"For by him were all things created, that are in heaven, and that are in earth, visible and invisible, whether they be thrones, or dominions, or principalities, or

powers: all things were created by him, and for him: And He is before all things, and by Him all things consist."

(Figure 2)

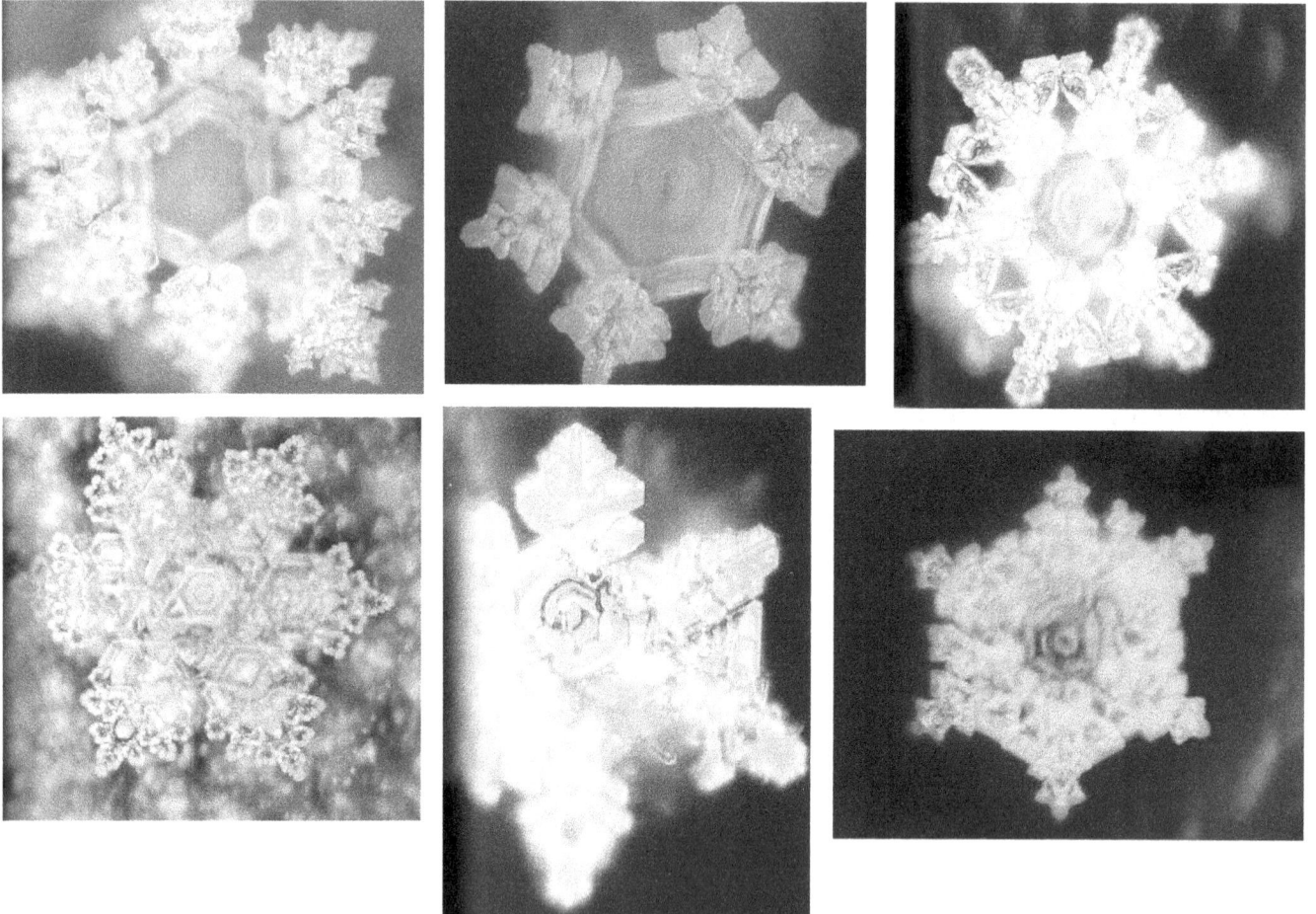

When the words *"You make me sick, I will kill you"* were spoken the crystals formed into this image. *(See photos - Fig. 3)*

(Figure 3)

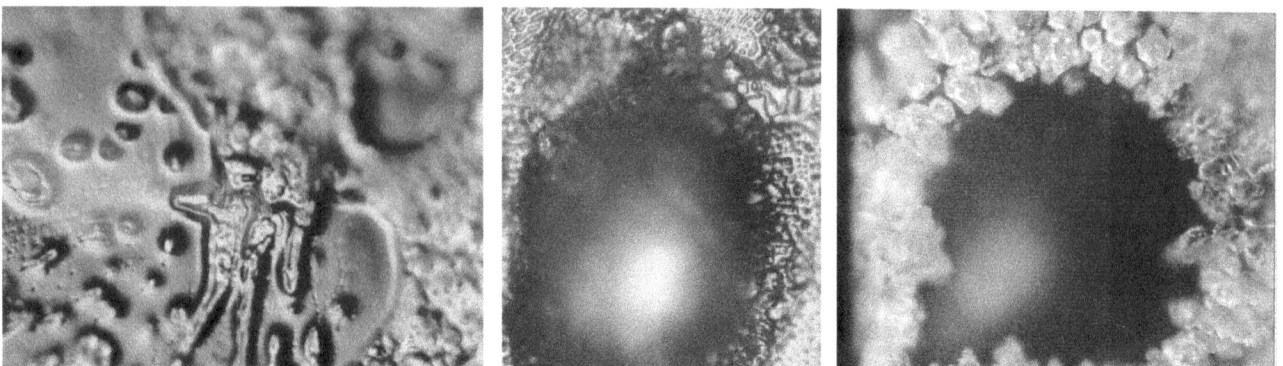

Mark 11:23 KJV
For verily I say unto you, That whosoever shall say unto this mountain, Be thou re-moved, and be thou cast into the sea; and shall not doubt in his heart, but shall believe that those things which he saith shall come to pass; he shall have whatsoever he saith.

When the words "Love and gratitude" was spoken this is what the crystals formed in-to—beautiful isn't it? *(See photos - Fig. 4)*

(Figure 4)

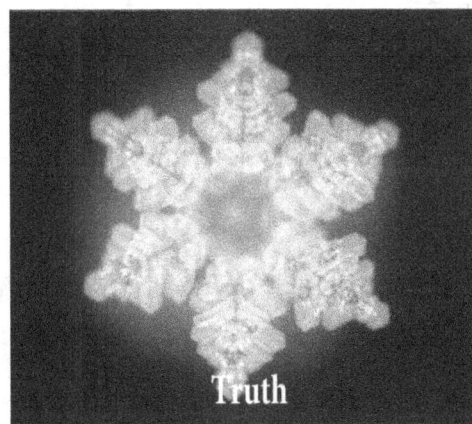

Psalms 19:14 KJV
"Let the words of my mouth, and the meditation of my heart, be acceptable in thy sight, O LORD, my strength, and my redeemer."

Finally when heavy metal music was played this is what the crystals formed into; a vor-tex of total confusion. *(See photo - Fig. 5)*

(Figure 5)

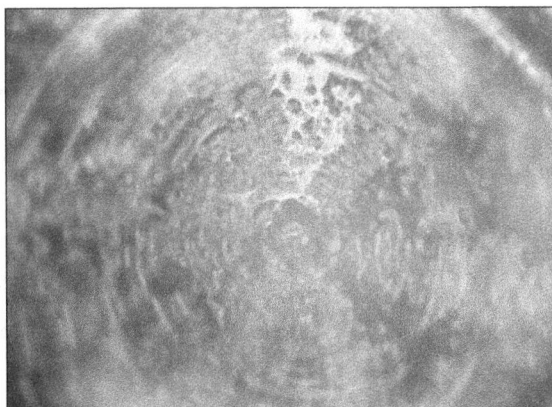

When you realize we are made up of mostly water: one must question, what are the words we speak; the songs we sing; and the music we listen to, doing to our bodies?

King David said *"set a watch over my mouth oh Lord."*

Psalms 141:3 KJV
Set a watch, O LORD, before my mouth; keep the door of my lips.

As we learn to manifest the nature of Jesus (His DNA) and our words become those of grace and love, we will begin to empower the Angels around us and begin to see Jesus in ways we have never seen Him before.

➔ Health is a Fruit of Righteousness ⬅

Luke 5:31-32 KJV
"And Jesus answering said unto them, They that are whole need not a physician; but they that are sick. I came not to call the righteous, but sinners to repentance."

Why did Jesus say this? Analyzing these two verses, we learn that Jesus said that the righteous are whole and the unrighteous [impenitent] are sick. Their sickness does not necessarily refer to any physical ailment alone, but specifically implies practiced or un-confessed sin (both conscious thought and subconscious thought). But it is intended to include psychosomatic illnesses as well, even demonic influences. In short, Jesus implied that *a converted sinner is a healed saint!* So by taking God at His Word, I must ask another question: why are there so many within the traditional church sick and dying prematurely? Obviously, the answer is: they are ignorant of spiritual truths of righteousness but also due to the fact they allow the anointing of the Holy Spirit, which abides within them, too remain dormant, so far as towards the complete conversion of their soul!

As the following verses attest, people become sick through their own ignorance and carnal obtuseness pertaining towards the multitudes of their iniquity! So, to reverse this trend of personal assault and condemnation, the remedy for this carnal tragedy is to obtain a working knowledge of specific truths of righteousness, whose influence transcends emotional torments, physical afflictions, traditions and societal influences! *Based upon a covenant relationship and by a constitutional necessity, the saint of God may choose to live in divine health or endure the affliction in grace, because a lifestyle of repentance reverses the iniquitous condemnation reverting it back towards and upon itself/ yourself!*

Biologically, it is said that our physical bodies regenerate brand new cells at the molecular level every six months or so. This total and complete regeneration denotes that our bodies were initially designed of God to live forever! It can't help but do so! However, if something is not done to correct future afflictions, then these new cells become tainted thereby perpetuating the affliction—such as in continued smoking. Because God created man's physical body to heal itself, by constitutional design, any and all illnesses must be eliminated from the body by way of the body's own defense systems! So, when a man allows his body to defend itself, it will eventually feel better because the body has been allowed to function, as it should.

In short, Jesus implied that a converted sinner is a healed saint! So by taking God at His Word, I must ask another question: why are there so many within the traditional church sick and dying prematurely?

For instance, if I were to accidentally cut myself, by design my body's defense systems would be activated to heal or regenerate the injured tissues, even at a molecular or cellular level. It will do this because it can't help itself but do so, for that is what it was designed to do! However, if I were to interfere with this healing process by neglecting my health through improper hygiene, then I suppress or hinder my body's defense systems and the cut could become infected, thereby complicating the healing process. In effect, I resist or frustrate this constitutional pre-existing condition. Since all truth is parallel, and since carnality is a preexisting affliction of the unregenerate soul, then repentance, as the spiritual defense system of the soul is also a preexisting, constitutional condition based upon a covenant relationship! Whereas, a man's body possesses preexisting defense systems to regenerate its health, likewise Almighty God has designed within the soul of man a spiritual defense system to regenerate its salvation, and that defense system within the soul is the conscience of the individual that alerts him of the need for it. So, whenever and as long as impenitent men reject repentance, they work against the constitutional design of their soul's basic need for salvation, even his own conscience, which is constantly urging him to come to repentance and be converted! *(cf. Ro 8:1-2; Heb 2:14; 1 Jo 3:8)*

Since people are in denial of their own carnality, they have no understanding of God's righteousness so far as it pertains towards their unatoned sin (iniquities). *(cf. Isa 22:14; Ro 3:10)*

Before anyone may understand righteousness, he first must acquire a working knowledge of his carnality, for therein he or she will find the Wisdom of the Just. The Apostle Paul said, "for this cause many are weak and sickly among you, and many sleep [are dead]." *(cf. 1 Co 11:27-30)* So the key to maintaining divine health is righteousness. A lifestyle of repentance promotes healing, health, restoration and complete wholeness, for these are also fruits of God's righteousness! *(cf. 1 Co 15:34)* What's more, Scripture tells us that through personal initiative, the saints of God are made the righteousness of God in Him, Jesus Christ because they aspire and seek after it. *(cf. Zep 2:1-3 AMP.; 2 Co 5:21; Mt 6:33)*

> *Proverbs 3:5-8 KJV*
> *"Trust in the Lord with all thine heart; and lean not unto thine own understanding. In all thy ways acknowledge Him, and He shall direct thy paths. Be not wise in thine own eyes; fear the Lord and depart from evil. It shall be health to thy navel and marrow to thy bones."*

➔ The Mercy of God as it Relates to Repentance ⬅

There is a difference between God's grace and His mercy! In short, Grace is a gift that is given albeit undeserved, while God's Mercy pertains to a deserved punishment that is withheld!

Jesus Christ became the recipient of God's wrath against man's rebellion and disobedience so that humanity would not. This then makes REPENTANCE essential for each individual if he/she chooses to be saved from such wrath. For without holiness, no one will ever see our Holy God. So Jesus Christ became God's propitiation (to make amends, and to reconcile man back to himself. Repentance then is a personal choice that denotes accountability, responsibility and obligation of a person who recognizes this spiritual truth; in other words, ownership! Through a lifestyle of repentance we are accountable to God and ourselves to be accountable for our conduct and behavior, even our thought life aka: Lie - Based Thinking.

Through a lifestyle of repentance, we become responsible for our actions, as well as our thoughts. And through a lifestyle of repentance, we have purposed ourselves to live a sanctified life! So forgiveness is required along with humility on our part and that as a personal choice!

Notes:_____

_____

_____

_____

_____

_____

_____

_____

_____

_____

_____

_____

_____

_____

_____

_____

_____

_____

_____

_____

_____

The WISDOM of The JUST

Notes:_____

Section 3

→ The spirit (word) of Error ←

The spirit (word) of Error Verses the Error of the Spirit (word)?

> *John 6:63 AMP*
> *"It is the Spirit who gives life [He is the life giver]; the flesh conveys no benefit whatever [there is no profit in it]. The words (Truths) that I have been speaking to you are spirit and life."*

> *1 John 4:1-6 AMP*
> *"Beloved, do not put faith in every spirit (word), but prove (test) the spirits to discover whether they proceed from God; for many false prophets (who say the same thing) have gone forth into the world and he who is not of God does not listen or pay attention to us. By this we know (recognize) the Spirit of Truth and the spirit of error."*

Now man is first a spirit who lives in a body and who possesses a soul. Both the spirit and the soul are intangible: that is, both are indistinguishable because they each are invisible/spirit. What's more, within the soul of man there exists a *spirit of his mind* that is also invisible. Now, since the mind is also spirit and is not the same as his spirit man, *all things that are logically perceived or mentally deduced are also spirit*! This would also include words, for as Jesus Christ Himself testified, *the Words* HE speaks are in fact *Spirit* Words (of Truth). Hence, it is reasonable too say also that all other *spirit words* that are not of God, are also spirit first and foremost.

Having said this, then it is also reasonable too say what is commonly called a *demon spirit* in all *actuality is an erroneous spirit word* that has attached itself to the spirit of one's mind as a lie, deception or delusion. Scripture indicates *the spirit of error.* (e.g., *Jas 1:14-16; also cf. 1 Joh 4:6*) I propose to you that it would be more precisely translated *the error of the spirit (word)*! This is because *the erroneous spirit word*, that so many false prophets (all spiritual leadership) do speak are tainted with either a denominational or personal bias, and is usually associated with a preferred doctrinal, financial or ideological slant.

The result being, inculcation (impression into the mind) of a dogmatic influence or a societal mind set which targets the spirit of the mind with *erroneous spirit words*; hence, the *error of the spirit* of the mind, and all because of words.

Now, what is commonly associated or believed to be *demon spirits are in fact erroneous spirit words* which have attached themselves to the spirit of the mind, for anything that is spirit is processed here, words included. These erroneous *spirit words* are *lies and other false pretenses* that have attached themselves to the memory bank of the mind and in this capacity; they become *iniquitous thoughts* that exalt themselves above the truth and the knowledge of God! *(cf. 2 Co 10:4-6; Ps 36:12)* It is for this reason that the Word of God is given and must be applied both logically and experientially if ever these *erroneous spirit words* are ever to be dislodged from our thinking! Once the Spirit (words) of Truth have entered into the area of the memory and has exposed the *lie - based thinking*, then and because of the Words of truth, the lie is forever expelled, dislodged, eradicated, etc.! Hallelujah!!!! However, so long as men choose to prefer their iniquitous thoughts in place of the Spirit of Truth, then such men are workers of their own iniquity (evildoers) and are *cowards* because they *practice their falsehoods*! *(cf. Ps 5:4-6, 94:16; Re 21:8,27)*

You see, up until now, I have placed more emphasis upon the Inerrant Word of God, which is too say that unless a certain topic, notion, idea or concept aligned to the literal Scriptural text, it would be disregarded immediately as incorrect, wrong or even blasphemous. However, in light of the above, the actual truth of the matter is that words are the least purveyor of Truth! This is due to the fact that words are very restrictive. Much is misunderstood, misinterpreted, manipulated (misused and abused). *Although the Word of God is truly stated, not all things stated are a statement of Truth!*

→ Man's Internal Justice System ←

(*Lu 18:1-8*: The parable of the Unjust Judge)
(See also *Ps 94:1-23* as the antithesis)

It is the intent of God for our minds be convinced of certain truths whether they are self-evident or not. These truths must therefore be either proven or demonstrated in such a manner so that our restless or chaotic minds will find peace—the peace which surpasses all worldly understanding. It is for this reason why cognitive knowledge must be correlated; that is too say, *logical knowledge must be supported with an experience, even an encounter to reinforce that knowledge.* Otherwise, without the experience or encounter of truth, the person remains lost in his or her inability to eradicate deceptive thoughts brought on by *precedence* caused by his *iniquity or her iniquitous thoughts.*

8⸺★

It is for this reason that the Word of God is given and must be applied both logically and experientially if ever these erroneous spirit words are ever to be dislodged from our thinking!

I have learned that when the mind has been presented with either proof or demonstration that is *True* to *Scripture*, to *Reason* and to *Life*, then it shall be *speedily* renewed! The *immediate outcome* shall be a welcomed change, even emancipation from iniquitous thoughts—lie - based thinking! The new-found liberty shall release the person to enjoy his/her freedom in God in the specific area of the lie, so that the character of the individual will reflect the corresponding conduct and behavior in Godliness!

Now, consider the volcano. Why do they exist and to what purpose do they provide or serve? Sometime ago while reading about volcanoes, the following reality came to mind. Planet earth has many volcanoes and just as each volcano has many subterranean lava tubes through which flows of magma travel to the surface and just as each volcano has its own magma boiling in a cauldron waiting to explode into the atmosphere, so likewise does every human being possess similar traits within their soul! *These physical volcanoes represent for us that which lies deep within each of us!* And just as volcanoes erupt, so likewise do we erupt whenever our life situation triggers our suppressed emotional magma!

Over the years, I have heard ministers preach on the parable of the *Unjust Judge* believing the main point to be that the Christian must hold on even with the tenaciousness of a bull dog. However with regards to this parable, I wish to introduce you to another perspective, which I do believe is accurate.

Now for the parable: (Observations)

(v 1)
Also [Jesus] told them a parable to the effect that they ought always to pray and not to turn coward (faint, lose heart, and give up). (cf. Heb 10:38-39)

"...*ought always to pray and not to turn coward.*" This denotes that *it shall require courage to face the true issues of your heart*, many of which you have avoided throughout your entire life! How often have you found yourself being challenged, panic-stricken or threatened by a particular event, situation, contact or scenario through which your *triggers* were pulled or your *buttons* were pushed? These life encounters triggered or pushed buttons to provoke your emotional outbursts thereby reinforcing certain existing bondages of your life. In verse 1, Jesus exhorts us to have the courage to confront *the skeletons in our closet*—even those dark shapes and shadows that cruise by! This courage is an intransitive term in that it is applicable across the board generally and not just specifically! In other words, Jesus does not relate courage to killing a lion only. Jesus does not speak of courage so far as it pertains towards those episodes in life that require immediate intestinal fortitude, such as in doing the right thing. This courage pertains also to those issues of the heart, *which most prefer to avoid!*

> *Psalms 90:8 KJ21*
> "*Thou hast set our iniquities before thee, [which are] those secret sins in the light of thy countenance.*"

And should a person choose to avoid, ignore or otherwise avert these wounds of his heart, (*thoughts of* iniquity) then that person is a *coward*, and remains an evildoer by *choice* and is *a worker of his/her iniquitous thoughts*! In effect, and through default, that person remains a *practitioner of falsehood*! (*cf. Ps 94:8, 16; Re 21:8, 27*)

⊶

> *I have learned that when the mind has been presented with either proof or demonstration that is True to Scripture, to Reason and to Life, then it shall be speedily renewed!*

(v 2)
He said, in a certain city there was a judge who neither reverenced and feared God nor respected or considered man.

The word City denotes the individual as a city on a hill. (*cf. Mt 5:14*) The *Unjust Judge* denotes *Lie - based thinking* (predominant iniquitous thoughts, even those attached to memories), as that fear or bondage which presides over one's thought life which does not revere God nor possess any regard for any man!

When you consider a courtroom, *the judge presides* over the trial, does he not? His presence ensures that all parties involved follow proper courtroom protocol of juris-prudence. Applying this example towards the Unjust Judge, *and your relationship to him [it], you should know that your (lie-based thinking) does preside over the affairs within your life and is incapable of having any regard or just consideration that would be in your best interest!* Hence, it is imperative that you personally take stock of your own iniquity and purpose to renew the spirit of your mind!

(v 3)
And there was a widow in that city that kept coming to him and saying, Protect and defend and give me justice against my adversary.

The word *Widow* denotes an unregenerate soul in the areas of the memory and the as-sociative lies that support it. According to the Strong's Concordance, the widow may be used literally or figuratively. So taking the figurative approach, *this widow is that area within your soul that feels forsaken, vulnerable, abandoned, insecure, selfish, etc.* The widow exists because she lost her husband. In like fashion the soul's widow exists because her husband (Jesus Christ/TRUTH) is not resident.

Judgment day honesty would obligate you to confess or admit that whenever you com-mitted a particular wrong doing, you did so because the *widow* within your soul pes-tered you to do so until you gave in to her demands! Is this not so?

"…who kept coming to him…"

This denotes at the very least a *bad habit* or worst still, an *addiction* or *bondage* does exist. It denotes the repetitive *preoccupation of iniquitous thoughts* that pertain to a par-ticular fetish! These pre-meditations of your carnal mind evince the very nature and characteristic of this neglected widow!

Do you understand this? For example, before a stalker kills his intended unsuspecting victim, he premeditates. He may start off with his fingers as an imaginary handgun. He then progresses to say a hair dryer that more closely resembles a handgun. After awhile, he purchases an actual weapon and rehearses (dry fires) this revolver at home in front of a mirror just as he has done all along with his previous improvisations. Finally, he is mentally prepared and at the ready to execute his intentions and commits murder, in the first degree *due to his premeditation*. Mind you this does not imply that all gun owners are of this mindset, but primarily the focus here is to generally imply that there are people of this disposition.

…Avenge me of mine adversaries…

This denotes a *false retaliation that manifest self-condemnation* which further victimizes the individual with destructive conduct and behavior against others such as seen in carnal addictions and emotional out bursts as these are cravings of the flesh.

Question: *Can an unjust judge decree righteous judgment?* The answer is NO! The unjust judge is incapable of righteous judgment for he does not reverence or fear God nor does he have any regard for man!

Jesus stated that a house divided against it self shall not stand! He spoke of Satan for Satan cannot divide Satan. *(cf. Mt 12:24-25; Mr 3:22-24; Lu 11:14-17)* He cannot *segregate himself from himself*, just as you or I could never separate our self from our self. In other words, wherever you may go, there you are! Having said this, it must be understood that *our iniquitous precedence are forever seeking a mind to live in*. This abode shall be a living host/body and it doesn't matter to these entities whether that host body is a person, an animal or possibly an insect! But they do prefer a person above the others; otherwise, *they continue to roam homeless (abandoned, intimidated, destitute and dispossessed), just as the widow feels.* Therefore, just as you or I would not intentionally do anything that would cause our expulsion from our homes and families, so likewise will the iniquity not do anything to cause its eviction? *(cf. Mt 12:43-45)* It is for this reason why they must be exposed for the parasites and vermin that they are, as people do coexist with vermin, parasites and pathogens each and every day. Is this not so?

Thank God for a healthy immune system! Even within any computer, viruses may be found! It is no different that any house would be bug-ridden with insects, rats or field mice.

(v 4)
"And for a time he would not; but later he said to himself, though I have neither reverence nor fear for God nor respect or consideration for man,"

Though I have neither reverence nor fear for God, nor regard for man…

This pertains to our *lie - based thinking* which neither concerns itself with the goodness of God or the benefit or welfare of man. All it is concerned with is itself! In other words, our lie - based thinking, would prefer to be left alone *to preside over the affairs in our life* which of course is based upon deception, condemnation and ridicule. These predominant lies could care less about righteousness, truth and integrity as these virtues are foreign concepts to them! These lies will allow a deceived person to kill, die or drive him to suicide just so long as the lies are left alone to do and be what they are characteristically.

(v 5)
Yet because this widow continues to bother me, I will defend and protect and avenge her, lest she give me intolerable annoyance and wear me out by her continual coming or at the last she come and rail on me or assault me or strangle me.

Yet because this widow troubeth me, I will avenge her...

This denotes that the false retaliation with which all men exhibit in their destructive conduct and behavior is the display of our perverted justice that serves to gratify our carnal desires! This gratification exists to enable the individual in his *pain management* that further leads to *bondage reinforcement*. This avengement is a self-imposed punishment for an actual or perceived wrong that is done by you or another (against you) and what's more your lie - based thinking is also a *false retaliation* on behalf of the lie itself just so that you could retaliate in a destructive manner!

So in this respect, it's a double whammy as that which is first unpleasant, but also is damaging to life, limb and property due to the consequences that follow. An excellent example of this would be the assassin John Hinckley who attempted to murder President Reagan in March of 1981. It is said that Hinckley was infatuated with the actress Jodie Foster. Because this actress refused Hinckley's advances towards her, he *abreacted* in that he released unconscious tension by talking about her rejections to himself and by reliving the events that caused his rejection. This type of soliloquy is premeditated and destructive self-talk. Do you understand?

lest she give me intolerable annoyance and wear me out by her continual coming:

Since the lie does not want to be evicted, it will dispense, as it were, a form of punishment to teach the individual that he/she must never attempt to be free of its deceit! The lie does not want to be *afflicted* with truth, because the truth means freedom from your iniquitous bondage as a spiritual emancipation from your Lie - Based Thinking! Hallelujah!!

rail on me or assault me or strangle me.

The lie is very concerned of its eviction! It does not want to be cast out because out there it roams afraid, restless and abandoned, just like any widow would feel. In Leviticus 23, Scripture speaks of the *Day of Atonement* and that *if a man does not afflict his soul, he shall be cut off from the camp.* The reason that a man must afflict his soul is because of that which exists as an affliction within his soul, namely his iniquity(s). *Therefore a lifestyle of repentance is the means of our soul's affliction (personal involvement and atonement) to assault the resident affliction (iniquity). Where the former is that which we must do, the later is that which must be eradicated!*

(v 6)
Then the Lord said, Listen to what the unjust judge says!

Hear what the unjust judge saith,

This denotes a mandatory attention to what we are listening to! In other words, our lie - based thinking is not of God who is the One, True Righteous Judge, but is of the unjust judge who fears not God nor regards the welfare of any man. *Soliloquy* is defined as *the act of speaking to your self while alone.* So listen to what you are saying and to what is being said within the framework of your mind! Is it lie - based or is your quiet talk founded upon scriptural truth?

(v 7)
And will not [our just] **God defend and protect and avenge His elect** *(His chosen ones), who cry to Him day and night? Will He defer them and delay help on their behalf?*

And shall not God avenge His own elect

This denotes that the goodness of Almighty God shall retaliate with a dispensation of righteous judgment and Truth to bring His saints to a lifestyle of repentance which shall illuminate the area of the deception, thereby exposing it for what it is—a lie from the pits of hell! For the entrance of God's Word brings light! *(cf. Ps 118:27, 119:130; Pr 6:23; Ro 4:1-4)* Unlike the perverted or distorted avengement from the unjust judge,

God's righteous judgment is a pure and righteous retaliation for He loves His people since He regards every man judicially and righteously! Whereas, the original question is, *Can an unjust judge dispense righteous judgment?*

The only true answer is that Almighty God is the righteous Judge who can and shall dispense righteous judgment, whether that judgment be for our good or for our condemnation. And if it is for our condemnation, we had better *know, understand and acknowledge* that He did not condemn us, but we condemned ourselves! *(cf. Joh 5:24)*

> *(v 8)*
> *I tell you, He will defend and protect and avenge them speedily, however, when the Son of Man comes, will He find [persistence in] faith on the earth?*

I tell you that He will avenge them speedily,

This denotes an abrupt and immediate change that takes place within the framework of the spirit of the mind and especially within the area(s) of the deception or lie - based thinking! This transformation shall be exhibited in a renewed countenance which is the after glow of a mind that has found rest and obtained peace in the Light of the Truth of God's Word that has illumined the specific area of the lie or pain. However, this shall only occur if we are willing. *(cf. Ps 79:8; Mt 21:42-45; 2 Co. 7:8-10)*

○—┬

So listen to what you are saying and to what is being said within the framework of your mind! Is it lie - based or is your quiet talk founded upon scriptural truth?

META: is the Greek word for repent. It means to renew, change, transform, metamorphous.

Nevertheless, when the Son of Man cometh, shall He find faith on the earth?

This denotes an appropriate concept of just what faith Jesus is speaking of. Specifically, that this kind of faith states that Almighty God shall do whatever He knows is necessary to accomplish so that His Justice, His Righteousness and Goodness would prevail in the affairs and wounded hearts of all men. Having said this then, it should be noted that this also pertains to our *leaning our entire personality [type] upon Him* and in doing so, that we allow/permit the Holy Spirit to do that which He knows He must do within our souls to expose deception, eradicate delusions and eliminate all lie - based thinking with His Word of Light, Truth and Righteous Judgment! Finally, *it is this kind of faith that shall set the captive free! It is this faith that we presently don't know, understand or acknowledge that will emancipate people from their afflictions and bondages! After all, the present faith that most people have is not the faith that they must know and it is precisely this faith that they don't have that shall set them free!*

In other words, denominational faith is not real faith, for denominational faith is a pseudo-faith that cows people down with religious tradition, bondage and churchianity, leaving them cattle minded and unknowledgeable with regards to their iniquitous thoughts! It is only as you separate yourself from this *erroneous spiritual influence* and allow yourself to investigate Scripture with a determined purpose to be set free from your iniquities on your own that you will ever be emancipated! It is the same adage: If you don't look after yourself, no one else will.

Opinions and Conclusions: I must conclude this thematic study with the following conclusions. *First,* as pertaining to the unjust judge—it is reasonable to assume that *any unjust judge is incapable of righteous judgment. Secondly,* that the perverted judgment that is dispensed from him (iniquitous thoughts) are also distorted. This carries over into the living condition (conduct and behavior) of the individual in that *the perverted judgment that is perceived to be righteous by the individual is in all reality a false retaliation against him and not for the benefit or welfare of that individual. Third,* that such *iniquity serves only to reinforce an existing bondage through the deception of pain management.* This explains to a large degree why people are so prone to impulsive conduct and behavior and explosive, emotional outbursts that serve only to gratify their carnal propensities.

→ From Paycheck to Paycheck and Battle to Battle ←

1 Samuel 17:47 NKJV
"And all this assembly shall know that the Lord saves not with sword or spear; for the battle is the Lord's, and He will give you into our hands."

We all live our respective lives from paycheck to paycheck. There is seldom a relief from the monthly tasks associated with this financial limitation. Consequently, domestic discord often arises due to the stresses of not having enough or barely making ends meet. In a similar manner, most people live out their livelihoods in a comparable way so far as their heart issues go. In other words, just as you might struggle month after month from paycheck to paycheck, you are also battling with the issues of your wounded heart from battle to battle. *And just as you may seldom acquire a financial relief during any particular month, so likewise do you seldom ever acquire genuine relief from the predominant triggers of your heart!* The Scripture above tells us ...*the battle is the Lord's*. He does not obtain victory through the use of swords or spears as men do. Rather, His victory is obtained solely on the foundation and the application of Truth, for Truth always triumphs over falsehood.

Paul said that there exists a war between and among our members. *(cf. Ro 7:23)* This warfare is a battle that we cannot ever hope to ever win in and of our own selves. To think so would be utter foolishness on our part. Perhaps you have thought for yourself that you can obtain the victory over something in your life through your own assertiveness? Maybe you have achieved a certain level of success because of your own efforts towards a particular vocation or endeavor. If this is the case, then you should know that all you have accomplished is to win a battle for the moment in your futile attempts at pain management of your wounded heart and soul.

The preceding insights exist to help cultivate your thinking on these essential topics at a forensic level. The purpose is to help you be prepared for what is to follow. Feel free to review any portion or all of the insights before you continue. It is important you *listen and not only hear* to this admonition! Otherwise, you will not *understand* the following Scriptures regarding your iniquity aka: Lie - Based Thinking.

Notes:_____

_____

_____

_____

_____

_____

The WISDOM of The JUST

Notes:_____

→ INIQUITY and INIQUITIES ←

And this infection of nature doth remain in them that are regenerated. (cf. the 39 Articles of the Church of England, Article 6)

Psalms 51:5 KJ21
"Behold, I was shapen in iniquity; and in sin did my mother conceive me."

Isaiah 22:14 KJ21
"And it was revealed in my ears by the Lord of Hosts, Surely, this iniquity shall not be purged from you till ye die, saith the Lord God of Hosts."

I think it is important in showing how compelling the logic of Scripture is in its record of the fall of Adam and the consequences to himself and his descendants. This is stated solely on this basis of the Council of Carthage in A.D. 412 condemning as heresy the three following propositions:

▶ (1) Adam was created mortal and would have died whether he had sinned or not.
▶ (2) The sin of Adam hurt only himself, and not all mankind.
▶ (3) Newborn infants die in the same state as Adam was in before the Fall.

We must assume the Council to have held, therefore, that Adam was not subject to death until he sinned; that the poison affected not only his own body but *was passed on by inheritance to all his descendants* and that no child of natural generation can ever avoid this physical defect and thus recover Adam's original state of deathlessness. Calvin expressed the view that sin is a "contagion":

"We are not corrupted by acquired wickedness, but do bring an innate corruptness from the very womb. All of us, therefore, descending from an impure seed come into the world tainted with the contagion of sin (iniquity)."

What makes iniquity, iniquity? I mean, since there is wickedness and goodness, and evil and sin, what makes any of these, what they are? In this thesis, I hope to show *what is known as a man's carnality is so because of the substance of his iniquity.* At the same time, I shall show that his iniquity is so because of the motives of his heart. A case in point would be the event in King David's life as found in *2 Samuel 24.* In verse one Almighty God instructed David to number the people. Upon learning of Israel's specific population, David's heart became filled with pride and his heart smote him. Although the deed of numbering was evil alone, it wasn't until David allowed and then entertained the titillation of the pride of life (as a motive of his heart) did it become his iniquity.

Scripture is replete with historical events between warring nations. These are in fact evil deeds and oftentimes, Almighty God did use other nations to correct His Chosen People. Although the evil nations were in fact evil, ultimately, Almighty God instructed them to attack and afflict Israel for their greater good. However, the problem of man's iniquity is founded upon the pride of heart that the conquering nations did emote. Had the conqueror left it alone as an evil deed accompanied with a proper motive of regret for having conquered another nation, then no iniquity would be attributed to them.

It is similar to the United States of America. American forces will conquer the evil, but America itself has never occupied that adversarial country with permanent occupation. Rather, America has always provided finances and other resources to rebuild the defeated nations.

It seems to me that in the New Testament, *justification* is applied only to deeds and *forgiveness* is applied only to motives. In other words, am I justified to do this or that deed and was my motive for these deeds appropriate? Evil is merely an event in its historical perspective--not in its moral perspective. When God addresses evil in Scripture, it is evil in the sense only that it appears to be an undesirable thing or event as a consequence of that evil done.

This distinction between evil and sin, and between goodness and righteousness; is interestingly pointed out when we remember that while we are never to tempt the Lord; that is too say—we are never to test His righteousness. *(cf. De 6:16)* We *are* however, invited too test for ourselves His goodness *(cf. Mal 3:10; Heb 4:16)*.

Similarly it is important to realize that it is *good works* and not *righteous works* that God foreordains for us to do. They only become righteous works when we choose *(cf. Eph 2:10; Php 2:13)*, and in precisely the same way it is *evil works* and not *wicked works* that God foreordains shall be done by the vessels of dishonor. These only become wicked when the doers of them take delight in them. An evil act in which a man takes delight becomes a *wicked one. It is the wickedness of a heart motive that is punished, not the act.*

But God's judgment is not based upon deeds at all; *it is based upon motives,* and therefore, whenever it is necessary for the fulfillment of His own purposes for some evil deed to be performed, in His omnipotence He can predetermine that it shall be so without in the slightest degree surrendering His right to condemn the doer *if he should take pleasure* in the evil. The evil things that we do are also used whenever God allows the consequences of them to result for our edification. Then such consequences are not to be thought of as punishments, but as being permitted by God in His graciousness that we might be made better. As F. L. Chappell (early American Dispensationalist) put it so pointedly:

"God's purpose in calling us to be laborers together with Him during this present age is not simply that the apparent work that He sets before us may be accomplished. It is, rather, that, in the accomplishment of this work we may be prepared for our chief and ultimate work in the age to come. For this reason the present age is disciplinary rather than executive. We are disciples, that is, students, more than we are workers at present."

The freedom man does have, lies only in the attitude (motive of heart) he takes toward what he does. *The sin of the world is not that it does not do the will of God, but that it does not choose the will of God. A sinner is not merely a sinner because he is a nonbeliever; he is a sinner because he chooses to reject the truth of God's Will for his life!*

The slave who freely chooses slavery remains a free man *(e.g., De 15:16-17)*. Our bondage to the will of God in Christ becomes a new freedom, for His will is perfect and our perfect obedience to His perfect will is our perfect freedom!

Below, I have conducted a thorough investigative word study of the words, INIQUITY and INIQUITIES (Falsehoods). In doing so, I have established a foundational understanding of each so far as they pertain to others and me universally. Having accomplished this, I can say that a basis for understanding is established which shall aid us in the scriptural import of what God's Word would have each of us to *know, understand and acknowledge* about our own iniquities. These iniquitous lies are *types that explain their function.* In fact, just as there are 7 categories of iniquity, so also there are 8 types of lies. Although, no longer in print, is used by permission. (*Source:* Chapter 6 of the Theophostic Prayer Ministry workbook by Ed M. Smith)

All lies are *falsehoods* (self-opinions) from which each of us base our individual lives. (*cf. Re 21:8, 27*) What's more, these lies are also *flesh hooks (See Fig. 6, p. 60)* that have attached themselves to our memories from which our misinterpretation in the present tense often occurs. For example, as a youth I was raised in a very hostile family environment. Although my birth certificate identifies my name to be Edward William Marr, I was raised to believe that my name was stupid, because dad repeatedly told me that *I was a stupid s.o.b., that there was nothing I could ever say that could possibly be of interest to others!* Consequently, I grew up believing this lie, for I *felt stupid!*

This episode of my youth under this destructive influence from my dad convinced me that I in fact was stupid, *because I believed what I felt!* This misinterpretation caused me to shy away from others, thereby compounding my immaturity.

Now, let's apply the *specific lie (type)* to my situation as well as the *specific lie (category)*. In doing so, I can say with great accuracy that *the type of lie* initially was *dad's lie about me* which I received as a youth. This lie type was for me *thematic and memory-linked* because I grew up into adulthood with this *theme of stupidity* because *the lie was attached to all my bad memories* involving dad. Secondly, I can *categorize* these lies as being *Fear based, Abandonment, Shame, Invalidation and Powerlessness* lies, because as a youth I *felt powerless* to do anything about dad, I *felt fear* because I did not want to be frightened or victimized by dad ever again, I *felt abandoned* and *betrayed*, I *felt shame* for myself, and I certainly *felt invalidated* because of my [perceived] stupidity.

⚷

The sin of the world is not that it does not do the will of God, but that it does not choose the will of God. A sinner is not merely a sinner because he is a nonbeliever; he is a sinner because he chooses to reject the truth of God's Will for his life!

Of particular interest is the expression *practicing falsehood(s)*, which is found in the Amplified Bible. For example:

Isaiah 59:13b AMPC
*"...speaking oppression and revolt, conceiving in and muttering and moaning **from the heart words of falsehood.**"*

Revelations 21:27 AMPC
*"But nothing that defiles or profanes or is unwashed shall ever enter it, nor anyone who commits abominations (unclean, detestable, morally repugnant things) or **practices falsehood**, but only those whose names are recorded in the Lamb's Book of Life." (cf. Ro 1:29-32; Col 3:22-23)*

Question: *What does Scripture mean to practice falsehood?* For most of us, any falsehood may be considered a lie and anyone speaking a lie is known as a liar. Is this not so? Therefore, *all liars would be considered to be practicing falsehoods*, at least on the surface. Well, let's take it deeper and apply this same thought towards our own *lie-based thinking*. In other words, *so long as we live our lives according to the script we believe about ourselves or that of another as rumors (vicariously) then we are all practicing falsehoods and since this is the case, then all of us would be workers of our own iniquity!* This is so because we believe what we feel! But a few questions are raised: 1) *What about all those who are long since gone and had never known this truth? 2) Are their names still recorded in the Lamb's Book of Life or were their names removed because of their iniquities? 3) Does God's amazing grace extend to those of us living in spite of our ignorance of our own iniquities?*

So let's compare Scriptures to find the answers to each of these questions. Now, I understand that whatever conclusion I have arrived at may differ from your conclusions. I suppose this difference would depend upon your ability or willingness to agree with the following Scriptures. Please accept the fact that I reviewed all 276 verses that contain the word *iniquity* as well as the 55 other verses that speak of *iniquities*.

Identifying the
➔ Different Types & Categories of Lies (Script) ⬅

Every Lie is a Script we have written for ourselves!

Eight Basic Types: *(Function)*

▶ **1)** *Script of Metamorphic Lies:* That which was true or at least possible or probable when a past event occurred is no longer true in the present. (Meta) Lies are implanted when people are acted upon against their will, causing them to feel over powered, out of control, weak and powerless. When the event occurred, their feelings were based on the truth, or at least were assumed to be true. But now as an adult, they are in control of their lives. They are no longer weak or powerless. *This means that what was once true is no longer true, even though it still feels true. Furthermore, just as a movie is scripted and makes us feel or affects us, so likewise do our falsehoods allow us to live out our lives in a false or imagined reality!*

▶ **2)** *Script of Cluster Lies:* Cluster Lies are found in memories that contain several distinct and separate lies. Each lie in the cluster will produce its own unique emotion and fall into its own separate category. Cluster Lies contain emotions that match the lies that are present. Cluster lies are several lies that reside within a single memory.

▶ 3) *Script of Clone Lies:* Are many unrelated memories that contain the same lie. A Clone Lie is created when an original lie is reproduced in later, secondary memory events. The original lie attaches itself to any new experience that is somewhat similar to the person's original experience of being wounded.

▶ 4) *Script of Memory-Linked Lies:* These lies are linked to each other but reside in separate memories, or in some cases, adjoining memories. They are unlike the Cluster Lies that are attached to the same memory. The Memory-Linked lie occurs when two or more lies are connected to each other but dwell in separate memories. There is usually an associated correlation between each memory. Whenever residual emotional pain remains within one memory, this residue is a good indicator of a lie that is attached to second memory that has yet to be resolved.

▶ 5) *Script of Guardian Lies:* This is a lie that is strategically positioned to block access to the root lies that are causing the havoc in a person's life. Guardian Lies are fundamental underlying beliefs a person learns through experience. A Guardian Lie does not always reside in the memory you are seeking to go to or in the one in which you are already working, but is positioned outside the memory to keep you from moving into the desired memory. Its source is usually found within another memory but also may have simply been learned over time through life. Guardian Lies are defensively positioned out in front of all the other memories to prevent access to the hidden lies.

<u>**Some examples of these falsehoods are:**</u>
- *"What I experienced is nothing compared to what others have had to deal with."*
- *"Right now is not a good time for me to deal with this."*
- *"It wasn't all that bad."*
- *"This TPM process will not work for me."*
- *"The pain is too much to deal with."*
- *"My past is behind me, now."*
- *"They didn't mean to hurt me."*
- *"I just need to put my past behind me."*

<u>**Dealing with Guardian Lies:**</u>
1) Identify the Guardian Lie in the person.

2) Ask the person how it feels to believe the lie.

3) Have the person focus on the Lie statement.

4) Ask the Lord to respond to this believe.

5) If the person receives truth, move toward the memory. If he does not, there is a reason. (Look for any presence of anger and deal with it first)

6) Have the person feel the emotions that are stirred up and request the person to be willing to move into the first memory.

<u>**Common Guardian Lies Include the following falsehoods:**</u>

- Time will heal.
- Forgive and Forget.
- *"I'll be Fine."*
- *"They never intended to hurt me."*
- *"My relationship with my wounder (perpetrator) is good now. If I bring up the past, I may put our relationship in jeopardy and lose what I have gained."*
- *"It is best just to leave well enough alone."*
- *"It probably wasn't as bad as I am making it out to be."*
- *"I have already dealt with this memory."*
- *"I really don't feel anything about it anymore."*

▶ **6)** *Script of Splinter Lies:* Are less threatening lies that sometimes crop up after the bigger, prominent lie has been removed from a specific memory. They are splinters from the fence post. Splinter Lies are distinguished by WHEN they surface and by the intensity of pain they produce. They are leftover lies.

▶ **7)** *Script of Osmotic Lies:* These are lies received by "OSMOSIS" or by absorbing it vicariously (by substitution). These lies are learned by observation from what we learn or observe in the life of others such as in behavior and attitudes.

▶ **8)** *Script of Thematic Lies:* A Thematic Lie is the consequence of a dysfunctional family system or lifestyle. It is the perpetual thinking of a family system, because the Lie was reinforced every day of his life. There are two types of Thematic Lies: Type A wounds which exist because of the absence of good things, and Type B wounds which are the BAD things that happen to us. Whenever there is a continual, on going flow of shaming, hurtful words and pain-inflicting behaviors acted out on a person, a theme develops.

Notes:_____

_____

_____

_____

_____

_____

_____

_____

_____

_____

_____

_____

_____

_____

_____

_____

_____

_____

_____

_____

Section 4

→ Eight Categories of Lies/Falsehoods: ←
(Nature or Character)

These eight categories of lies are umbrella lies under which all other lies are found or vise versa.

Falsehood #1 ~ Fear Lies: Most Fear Lies are Metamorphic in type. They originate in those events containing true danger. But the problem is that although the dangerous event may be long since past, the continued perception that we are still in danger is false. What was true previously is no longer a true statement or reality present.

Falsehood #2 ~ Abandonment Lies: When a person has memories of being forsaken, deserted, left alone, unprotected, or unloved. Also feelings of rejection, being shunned or unnoticed are included in this category. Whereas, a Fear Lie is about impending doom or harm, an Abandonment Lie has more to do with being isolated and alone.

Falsehood #3 ~ Shame Lies: Shame is the consequence of people doing something, causing something, or participating in something they believe to be wrong. They feel shame or guilt because they perceive themselves to be at fault. It does not matter if they are really innocent. It is their belief that they have done something wrong that causes the shame and guilt. Shame and guilt often accompany self-condemning lies.

Falsehood #4 ~ Taintedness Lies: Whereas the Shame Lie is rooted in self-condemnation, the Taintedness Lie creates a feeling of shame, not because something that I did was wrong but because something wrong was done to me. *I feel shameful, nasty, and dirty because I was raped, molested, touched, violated or hurt.*

Falsehood #5 ~ Hopelessness Lies: Hopelessness Lies tell people to give up, since there is no hope of ever being free or getting better or finding a way out of the situation. The Hopelessness Lie is attended by despair, depression, and lethargy. Hopelessness Lies often drive people towards suicide or possess suicidal tendencies.

Falsehood #6 ~ Invalidation Lies: God made parents responsible for providing their children with the truth about their worth. When children are not validated, they come to false conclusions about themselves. Hurtful criticism and condemnation go deep into children's hearts and minds. Invalidation Lies are clustered with Hopelessness Lies.

Falsehood #7 ~ Powerlessness Lies: Found in the memories of people, who have been constrained an unable to act. The Powerlessness Lie is different from the Hopelessness Lie. A person may believe that he is Powerless and although he sees the way out and knows what must be done, he believes that he is unable to act or do anything about the situation. Whereas, a Hopelessness Lie sees no way out at all. Due to forceful encounters of abuse, molestation or violation of personhood such person believes the Powerlessness Lie because that is how he is made to feel.

Falsehood #8 ~ Confusion Lies: Confusion Lies are common among adults who report having been wounded before they were old enough to understand what was happening to them later in life, this Lie may recur in the form of overwhelming confusion. As adults, these people will be unable to make sense out of a current circumstance or understand why it is happening. Often, their inability to articulate themselves occurs.

So let's begin with a basis of understanding of just what or how the Scriptures define or describe *iniquity* and *iniquities*. The following text will provide us a foundation of mutual interpretation from which we may acquire a common meaning, okay? Upon reviewing the following, I promise you that you will never again consider either word to be just one of those awkward biblical expressions. On the contrary, you will have acquired specific knowledge so much so that you shall *know, understand and acknowledge your iniquity* for yourself and hopefully be liberated from these falsehoods of deceptive lies and other stratagems of deceit! *Encarta Dictionary* defines *iniquity and iniquities* to be nouns and are defined or described to be: "great injustice or extreme immorality, a grossly immoral act, wickedness, evil, sin, vice, injustice, crime" *I wish to further define iniquity to be representative of the motives of heart.*

The *Strong's Exhaustive Concordance* defines or describes both as follows:

▪ *Iniquity* is defined as: Hebrews Reference #5753: A-vah means: to crook, lit or fig. –do amiss, bow down, make crooked, commit iniquity, pervert, (do) perversely, do wickedly, do wrong, trouble, to overthrow. Ref #5771: avon means: (moral) evil:--fault, iniquity, mischief, punishment (of iniquity), sin.

▪ *Iniquity* is defined as: Greek Reference #458: anomia means: illegality, i.e. violation of law or (gen) wickedness—iniquity, transgression of law, *unrighteousness*. Ref. #459 anomos means: lawless, not subject to the law, wicked:--without law, lawless, transgressor, unlawful, wicked.

Romans 3:10-11 KJV
"There is none that understands, There is none that seeks after God."

Matthew 6:33 KJ21
"But seek ye first the kingdom of God and His righteousness..."

1 Corinthians 15:34 KJ21
"Awake to righteousness! For some have not the knowledge of God and I speak this to your shame."

▪ **What does Scripture say about Iniquity?** Scripture has much to say about iniquity! In fact, there are *276 Scripture passages* that address *iniquity* directly and another *55 passages* that speak of *iniquities*! This does not include the multiple hundreds of additional passages that directly address *wicked, wickedness, transgression(s), transgressor(s), self-righteousness*, etc. In the addendum you will find all these powerful passages for your reference as you read this book.

▪ **Who has Iniquity and from whom or where did they come?** Every man ever born has iniquity within the faculties of his mind. It is for this reason why or how the carnal mind exists. *(cf. Ec 3:18; Ro 8:5-8; 2 Co 3:14-16)* Carnality and iniquity were born on the occasion of Adam's fall from grace in the Garden of Eden. In effect, he became a living host of the volatile seed—iniquity and every succeeding generation that followed have been infested by it! Look at it this way. Just as *two peas have a pod* and just as any *seed has its husk*, so likewise does *iniquity have a shell of carnality! So then to expose the peas, the seeds and our iniquity (the pod or husk) the shells of each must be broken open and this includes the shell of our carnality! As has been said, every seed has or possesses life. Life is found within the seed. So likewise, the shell of carnality possesses the seed of that gives life to our transgressions...our iniquity!*

▪ **What is Iniquity?** Whereas carnality is a general expression, iniquity is a more specific articulation. Iniquity is more than carnality or to be carnally minded. *Where carnality could be considered a husk, Iniquity is like a spiritual pathogen within this husk* *that attaches itself to the seedbed of our memories that are cherished treasure, whether for the good or the bad, within our heart. (cf. Mt 12:34-37)*

Just as a puppy would be infested with heartworms unless treated, and just as there are those diseases that do target the cardiovascular system of man, so likewise does iniquity target the heart of all men. This means that man's iniquity is an actual degenerative heart condition that mandates an immediate corrective procedure and *a lifestyle of repentance is this procedure!*

⚷

God made parents responsible for providing their children with the truth about their worth. When children are not validated, they come to false conclusions about themselves. Hurtful criticism and condemnation go deep into children's hearts and minds.

▪ **Where does Iniquity reside?** As stated, iniquity resides within the heart of every man. But iniquity also resides as *a throne* over nations, communities, families and individuals. *And since man's iniquity is a throne, its scepter (sword of state) is as a rod of authority, which imposes itself within the fabric of societal mindsets!* Much like a computer's memory bank (card) may be exposed for all the data con-tained therein, so likewise does the spirit of the mind possess a memory-bank in both the conscious and subconscious faculties of the mind. It is here where our iniquities dwell or exist, especially within the subconscious theater. *(See Fig. 7, p. 83)*

▪ **When or at which time or season does iniquity exist?** Scripture speaks of the time when kings went to war. *(cf. 2 Sa 11:1) There is a throne of iniquity and as such this throne represents and is that seat of dominion of our carnality!* Whereas, a man's life throughout the days of his living is a time for repentance, so likewise does iniquity take its opportunity in and throughout the days of every man's life. Herein, the purpose of repentance is established by reason of iniquity. *(cf. Zep 2:1-3 AMP)*

▪ **Why does Iniquity exist?** Iniquity first and foremost exists because of the fall of man. Secondly, iniquity continues to exist within the heart of every man born for we all have been conceived in this un-atoned pathogen. This means that so long as any man chooses to ignore or reject the truth of the existence of his iniquity, he perpetuates the governing seat of his iniquity within his wounded heart!

▪ **How does iniquity exist?** Iniquity exists because the heart of man is wicked, even wounded. Therefore, iniquity finds its home within this seedbed (hearts) of impenitent men thereby wounding millions even billions of people *as the greatest weapon of mass destruction.*

➜ Nomenclature of Iniquity ⬅
The Realm of Spiritual Wickedness in High Places as the Principalities of Life
(Ephesians 6:12)

Below, I have found in Scripture 7 categories or classifications of iniquity. Collectively, each category provides a composite of our iniquity, which infers its nature or characteristic. Of interest, I wrote the following insight while at church about 20 years ago where in I itemized each falsehood spoken of in *Ephesians 6:12.* They are altogether secular and worldly! *Principalities* are ideologies, *Powers* are rules and regulations, *Rulers* are enforcement and *Spiritual Wickedness* is oppression and bondage. These also apply to the church leadership, wherein high level church ministries are opposed at the higher level of such leadership!

▶ **1)** *The Thoughts of Iniquity:* Are those conscious and subconscious premeditations of the mind that I refer to as *Lie - Based Thinking.*

▶ **2)** *The Throne of Iniquity:* As having dominion over every man.

▶ **3)** *The Scepter of iniquity: vs. the Scepter of Righteousness* (Sword of State) each scepter is the emblem of power or authority. This denotes that men live ignorantly *under the authority* of their iniquity or they may live *in authority* over their Lie - Based Thinking. The choice is always ours. *(cf. Ro 6:19)*

Let me digress here to explain an *ORB*. By definition, an *orb* is a globe, sphere or planet. Often, an orb is fashioned onto the top of a scepter and it denotes authority, rulership. But consider this… The cross upon which Jesus Christ died was/is Almighty God's Orb because planet earth is created as a globe and is therefore a sphere. His Orb represents for all of humanity the freedom to choose to live our lives in His righteousness and Truth! Hallelujah !!!

▶ 4) *The World of Iniquity* denotes all perceptions of self, others, life and God based upon our lie - based thinking.

▶ 5) *The Workers of Iniquity:* vs. coworkers (laborers) either with Christ or in opposition to. *(cf. 1 Co 3:9)*

▶ 6) *The Reward of Iniquity* vs. having Respect unto the recompense of the reward. *(cf. Heb 11:24-26)*

▶ 7) *The Bond of Iniquity:* vs. the Bond of Peace *(cf. Eph 4:3)*

Everything that has ever been designed, invented or created has one thing in common. Each one had its origin as a thought or an idea! Consequently, our thoughts become containers, as it were, in which the treasures of our heart are contained. These treasures are in effect principalities; whether they are of God or of Satan. Obviously then, Godly thoughts pertain to those things of God while iniquitous thoughts pertain to deceptions of Satan; for he is the father of lies and all liars!

By principality I mean to say that it is not just a territory ruled by a prince or a tyrant, but it is also a position or jurisdiction as the seat of authority within the framework of a person's mind.

Revelations 21:27 AMPC
*"But nothing that defiles or profanes or is unwashed shall ever enter it, nor anyone who commits abominations (unclean, detestable, morally repugnant things) or **practices falsehood**, but only those whose names are recorded in the Lamb's Book of Life."*

▪ **The Thoughts of Iniquity:**
Isaiah 32:6 AMPC
*"For the fool speaks folly and **his mind plans iniquity: practicing profane ungodliness and speaking error concerning the Lord,** leaving the craving of the hungry unsatisfied and causing the drink of the thirsty to fail." (cf. Mt 5:6; Joh 7:37-39; Re 21:27)*

Isaiah 59: 7 AMPC
*"Their feet run to evil, and they make haste to shed innocent blood. **Their thoughts are thoughts of iniquity;** desolation and destruction are in their paths and highways."*

First off, man's iniquity deprives the soul of Godly satisfaction! This is because the soul has a genuine need for salvation and truth! When any man chooses to neglect his soul of Almighty God's salvation according to Scripture that man actually fails to feed his soul with spiritual food and drink! *(cf. Joh 6:47-58)* Although he may seek contentment in his iniquity, as a junk food addict, this contentment in all reality is a *false retaliation,* which further desolates *as that which makes him feel sad or lonely* thereby escorting the soul, pushing it along towards eternal destruction and condemnation! (Remember, we believe what we feel.)

As previously stated, any thing designed, created, invented or made has its original concept as a thought. This includes regimes, kingdoms, domains and political engines as well as societal and individual mindsets. Each had its origin as a *concept of intention* within either the mind of God or the mind of man. With regards to the iniquitous thoughts, suffice it to say also that these beliefs had their conceptualization within the mind of their father—Satan himself, for he is the father of lies, is he not?

⊶

Everything that has ever been designed, invented or created has one thing in common. Each one had its origin as a thought or an idea! Consequently, our thoughts become containers, as it were, in which the treasures of our heart are contained.

I mentioned domains. Just as a kingdom is the domain of a king, so likewise there exists the domain of self! *Selfdom* therefore is that which consists of our entire personality (type) as well as the tri-unity of our personhood (Spirit, Soul and Body). Especially, since *selfdom* includes the spirit of the mind in each of the four faculties (will, understanding aka: the will, intelligence, conscious, and reasoning) which do exist.

- **The Throne of Iniquity:** *(Spiritual Wickedness in High Places)*

    Psalms 94:20 AMPC
    *"Shall the **throne of iniquity** have fellowship with You—they who frame and hide their unrighteous doings under [the sacred name of] law?"*

This Scripture implies that under the guise of religion, all men are attempting to usurp

God's determined will and purpose for all men everywhere and for all times to come to faith and repentance! Instead, men have conjured up a religious tradition by substituting God's terms and conditions for salvation with another gospel! *(e.g., Ga 1:6-7)*

Every kingdom has a throne, and that kingdom would not exist without those subjects over or upon whom a kingdom rule is established, whether righteous or not, This world supports this truth in that *every sovereign nation has its own throne or kingdom rule,* do they not? Presently, North Korea and Iran are two hot spots of iniquity due to the trouble each leader is mischievously involved with. Their aspirations to acquire nuclear weapons has caused other nations to stand at a stage of high alert, even with strong promises of severe military retaliation should these two nations continue with their unwarranted deeds of nuclear proliferation.

Now these kingdoms each have a throne from which an established rule of law is dispensed towards those subjects or citizens within these kingdoms. All citizens then are obligated to comply with the laws of the land, whether righteous or not. These two kingdoms are closed societies; in that they are intentionally segregated from the rest of the world. In doing so, the citizens remain ignorant of outside intentions for their benefit, thereby fostering the only societal mind set that is most conducive to the existing regime. *This in itself is a throne of iniquity and all those who reside under such authoritative influence are prone to iniquitous thoughts perpetrated by those in the governing regimes.* This is because the lie - based thinking attaches itself to the wounded hearts of one and all! Even those in power or authority are *wounded* themselves and their conduct and behavior against others *is indicative of their own unacknowledged heart felt festering wounds,* thereby continuing an unbroken cycle of despair and heartache! According to Scripture, Death is the only physical remedy for man's iniquity in the natural! However, through the power of the Holy Spirit, anyone may be set free from their own oppression brought on by their own iniquitous thoughts! The choice is always yours!

> *Isaiah 22:14 KJ21*
> *"And it was revealed in mine ears by the Lord of Hosts, **surely this iniquity shall not be purged from you till ye die**, saith the Lord God of hosts."*

And lest you think that you are superior just because you live in a free nation, think again! You and I would be no different than those poor citizens who are ensnared and entrapped in these segregated countries. As pertaining to families and individuals, *iniquity follows the same route of domination or authoritative rule as a lie - based principality!*

- **The Scepter of Iniquity:**

  Psalms 125:3 AMPC
  "For the scepter of iniquity shall not rest upon the land of the [uncompromisingly] righteous, lest [unless] the righteous (God's people) stretch forth their hands to iniquity and apostasy."

Whereas, every king would possess a scepter as a symbol of his ruler-ship and authority, so to then does *the throne of iniquity possess a scepter of deceit, the authority of which would be evident in the character of the individual so bound by such lie - based thinking!* This scepter of iniquity would become for the impenitent, a *sword of state* that infers that he lives his life willingly under the authority of his iniquitous thoughts! Just as David approached Goliath carrying a stick, *(cf. 1 Sa 17:40-43)* so likewise does every man possess within his heart a *rod of deceit* which for him is his *sword of state!* Only thing is that *this sword* will decapitate any man who chooses not to come to repentance for his iniquities! In effect, that man commits spiritual suicide! *(cf. Pr 18:9 AMP)* And let me stress that since iniquitous thoughts are a daily event for everyone, *a lifestyle of repentance is necessary to cultivate throughout the days of our living!*

- **The World of Iniquity:**

  James 3:6 AMP
  "And the tongue is a fire. [The tongue is a] **world of wickedness** *set among our members, contaminating and depraving the whole body and setting on fire the wheel of birth (the cycle of man's nature), being itself ignited by hell (Gehenna)."*

According to this Scripture, the untamed tongue of impenitent men is a *world of iniquity* that is set in the midst or among our members. This verse also implies that this *world of iniquity* contaminates and depraves the whole body (of absolute, divine truth) and sets on fire the cycle of man's wicked nature, since it is ignited by hell.

The members, in my opinion, are a reference towards the four faculties of the mind that are as follows: *will, intelligence, conscience and reasoning.* Together these faculties comprise all cognitive and emotional aspects of a personality (type), and consist of the lie - based thinking that resides therein.

- **The Workers of Iniquity:**

  Psalms 94:8, 16 AMPC
  "Consider and understand, you stupid ones among the people! *And your [self-*

*confident] fools, when will you become wise? Who will rise up for me against the evildoer? Who will stand up for me against the **workers of iniquity?***"

Scripture repeatedly indicates that any man who chooses not to acknowledge the Truth of God so far as it relates towards the lie - based thinking of his wounded heart, or fails to be renewed in the spirit of his mind shall be considered a worker of iniquity! Furthermore, Scripture teaches that Almighty God hates all evildoers (workers of iniquity)

...through the power of the Holy Spirit, anyone may be set free from their own oppression brought on by their own iniquitous thoughts! The choice is always yours!

Psalms 5:4-6 AMP
"For you are not a God who takes pleasure in wickedness; No evil [person] dwells with you. The boastful and the arrogant will not stand in your sight; You hate all who do evil. You destroy those who tell lies; The Lord detests and rejects the bloodthirsty and deceitful man."

- **The Reward of Iniquity:**
  Acts 1:18 AMPC
  *"Now this man obtained a piece of land with the [money paid him as a] **reward for his treachery and wickedness...**"*

  Hebrews 11:26 AMPC
  *"He [Moses] considered the contempt and abuse and shame [borne for] the Christ (the Messiah Who was to come) to be greater wealth than all the treasures of Egypt, for he looked forward and away to the **reward (recompense).**"*

In *Acts 1:16-20* Scripture teaches that Judas Iscariot was not just a worker of iniquity but his just reimbursement for his iniquity (evil heart felt motivation) was also his just reward! In other words, as any worker expects to be paid his salary or wage, *so likewise can any worker of iniquity expect to be reimbursed as a payment that is due him as a reward for his iniquity.* This reward does not just pertain towards life hereafter, but it also pertains to life experiences in the here and now! Whereas, the iniquitous thought exists to satisfy the urges of carnality, as an antithesis, when a man has come to repentance, he acquires a respect unto the recompense of His reward. This reward is the lawful payment or benefit in absolute truth and righteousness as a divine gratuity, even a spiritual endowment. *The fact that a penitent man respects the recompense of the reward means that he has placed a value on the spiritual things of God over the preference of carnal mindedness and his iniquitous thoughts!*

- **The Bond of Iniquity:**
  Acts 8:22-23 AMPC
  "**<u>So repent of this depravity and wickedness of yours</u>** *and pray to the Lord that, if possible, this <u>**contriving thought and purpose of your heart may be removed and disregarded and forgiven you.**</u> For I see that you are in **the gall of bitterness and in a bond forged by your iniquity** [to fetter souls]."*

  Ephesians 2:14 AMPC
  "For He is Himself our peace (our bond of unity and harmony). He has made us both [Jew and Gentile] one [body], and has broken down (destroyed, abolished) the hostile dividing wall between us."

Iniquity is that wickedness (bitterness) within a wounded heart that serves only one destructive purpose, to snag a lie as an encumbrance to a wounded heart! This falsehood is a contriving thought (even premeditation) with the sole intention of imbedding a root of bitterness (bondage) which has been forged by the iniquitous thought. This bond is as an attachment (as a flesh hook, *(See Fig. 6, p. 60)* that fastens a lie to a wounded heart's memory; the lie then serves as the foundation for personal beliefs that often appear as emotional outbursts, even acts of violence against self and others.

Now the contrast to this *Bond of Iniquity* is that *Bond of Peace* (Who is Jesus Christ Himself and the harmonious relationship of being unified with Him). In doing so, specific iniquitous thoughts are captured and thrown down—unable to arise ever again, because the mind's *cognitive veil has been perforated. (See Fig. 7, p. 83)*

  Psalms 36:11-12 KJ21
  "Let not the foot of pride come against me, and let not the hand of the wicked remove me. There are the workers of iniquity fallen: they are cast down and shall not be able to rise."

(Figure 6)

**ʃ = Flesh Hooks - Iniquitous Thoughts
Lie-based Thinking**

**Shell of Carnality
Pod to Pain**

**Stripes for Iniquity:
Pr 19:29; Ps 89:32; Is 53:5**

**Lies,
Falsehoods,
Deceptions,
Delusions**

MEMORIES

**Cracks denote
Wounds
Brokeness
Crevices
Crannies**

**Isa 59:2-18
Eze 18:20-32
Ps 51:6-19
2 Co 7:8-10 AMP
Lu 18:1
Re 21:8, 27**

[Stone Cold Heart]

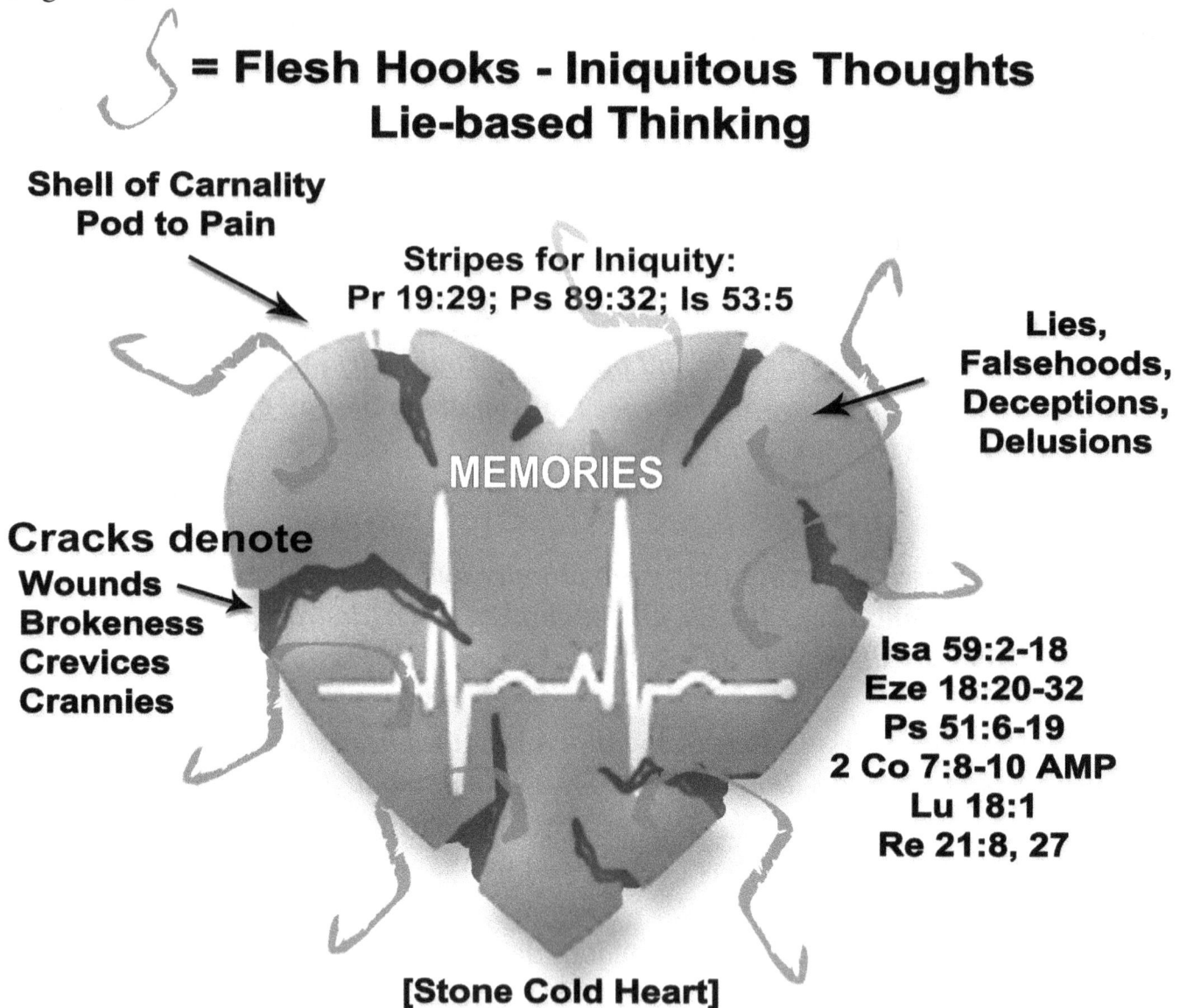

→ The Effects of Iniquity (Breaking the Fourth Wall) ←

Once again, I would like to express "Breaking the Fourth Wall". It is an expression often found in the entertainment industry. It means *to suspend your disbelief.* In other words, since most theatrical events are fiction, for the time that you enjoy the movie, television, or theatrical performance, and although you know logically that the performance may not be based upon reality or truth, you willingly allow yourself to *suspend your disbelief* and in doing so, your mind embraces the (deception) performance. *Applying this towards our iniquity, the premeditations of our deception as iniquitous thoughts eventually break down the fourth wall within our minds.* Once this wall has been breached, titillations take place within our minds because we have been touched ever so lightly with deceptive theatrics! It is for this reason why and perhaps how any man or woman commits crimes against society as well as against themselves, even God's Word!

You can imagine this when you consider that we think in pictures. Across the theater of your mind is played a consistent theme or plot of your life. And as any theme would have a story line, the lyrics of your life are encoded into the thematic deceptions that are your iniquities. *Applying this to real life scenarios, since we think in pictures and our imaginations go beyond the spiritual into our living, then the activities in our life mimic that which we see within the theater of the spirit of our mind.* Here is what Scripture has to say about this concept.

Ezekiel 22:9 KJV
"In thee are men that carry tales to shed blood; and in thee they eat upon the mountains; in the midst of thee they commit lewdness."

In this passage, the tales speak of *the suspension of disbelief* within the minds of those men who gave themselves over to the fictions, the fantasies, and the falsehoods. They in effect become *practitioners of their own falsehoods!*

Proverbs 18:8 AMPC
"The words of a whisperer or talebearer are as dainty morsels [titillations]; they go down into the innermost parts of the body."

1 Timothy 1:3-7
*"...that you might warn and admonish and charge certain individuals not to teach any different doctrine. Nor to give importance to or occupy themselves with legends (fables, myths) and endless genealogies, which foster and promote useless speculations and questions rather than acceptance in faith of God's administration and divine training that is in faith...**But certain individuals have missed the mark on this very matter [and] have wandered away into vain arguments and discussions and purposeless talk.** They are ambitious to be doctors of the Law (teachers of the Mosaic ritual), but they have no understanding either of the words and terms they use or of the subjects about which they make [such] dogmatic assertions."*

Ezra 9:6-8 AMPC
*"Saying, O my God...for **our iniquities have risen higher than our heads** and our*

guilt has mounted to the heavens. Since the days of our fathers, we have been exceedingly guilty and for our willfulness…And now, for a brief moment, grace has been shown us by the Lord our God Who has left us a remnant to escape…that our God may brighten our eyes and **give us a little reviving in our bondage.***"*

Psalms 38:4 KJV
"For mine iniquities are gone over my head: as a heavy burden, they are too heavy for me." (cf. 2 Co 10:5-6; Isa 57:17)

Our iniquities must be suppressed, and the prescribed manner of suppression is God's experiential Way, Truth and Life (style) of repentance, for in it is found the knowledge of salvation! *(cf. Lu 1:76-77)*

This *experiential truth* is not the logical head knowledge, which we all have, nor is it Scripture memorization; rather, it is the encounter of God's truth that has been experienced as an actual event within the specific area of your iniquity. This also pertains to *experiential knowledge*, which refers to the actual event that embodies the lies associated to that eventful memory. Therefore, this *experiential knowledge* must be dealt a fatal blow with *experiential truth*!

Nehemiah 9:2 AMPC
"And the Israelites **separated themselves from all foreigners** *and stood and confessed their sins and their iniquities of their fathers."*

My iniquity is as a foreign object within my soul! Therefore, just as a surgical operation may be required to remove an actual foreign object from within my physical body, so likewise is there a key necessity that exists which requires that my iniquities *(as those foreign objects)* be removed from the recesses of my mind that renders it carnal.

Psalms 32:5 AMPC
"I acknowledge my sin to You, and **my iniquity I did not hide.** *I said, I will confess my transgressions to the Lord [continually unfolding the past till all is told]—then You [instantly] forgave me the guilt and iniquity of my sin.*

Hebrews 10:17 AMPC
"He then goes on to say, and their sins and their lawbreaking (iniquity) I will remember no more." (Parenthesis mine)

Psalms 119:130 AMPC
*"The entrance and **unfolding of Your words** give light; **their unfolding** gives understanding (discernment and comprehension) to the simple."*

Lie upon lie, memory after memory! All of us have a recollection of episodes, events, seasons and times of injuries that we all have either endured, weathered, inflicted upon another or survived. Our survival does not however equate to wholesome living because all of us are as the walking wounded! Repentance is given to all men by Almighty God so that throughout all the days of our living we would come to repentance and *unfold our past exposing its lies one by one.* You see, the Holy Spirit will give to us the *unfolding Word of His grace thereby allowing us to unfold our past and the iniquities associated!* Truly, Almighty God has a remedy for man's carnal tragedy! Hallelujah!!!

Psalms 40:12 AMPC
*"For innumerable evils have compassed me about; **my iniquities have taken hold on me that I am not able to look up. They are more than the hairs of my head** and my heart has failed me and forsaken me."*

Whereas, a haircut reduces the amount of hair and whereas the follicles still remain, though the head may be shaved to the bone, in similar fashion man's carnality must be kept under because the follicles of our iniquities still exist within our wounded heart.

Baldness represents repentance and in this sense repentance becomes the shears used to cut out iniquities, one iniquity at a time for each and every memory. *(cf. Mic 1:16)* The vanity of most men with regards to their hair loss presupposes their iniquitous thoughts and for this repentance remains balderdash! (Nonsense) Also, this verse states that there are a *multitude of iniquities*, just as there are multitudes of hair! Only God knows the number of the hairs on our head. So likewise does He also know the number of iniquities within the wounded heart of each and every man! This is why a wounded heart fails and a person feels forsaken, abandoned, rejected, etc.

Psalms 90:8 AMPC
*"Our iniquities, **our secret heart** and its sins [**which we would so like to conceal even from ourselves**], You have set in the [revealing] light of Your countenance."*

Psalms 19:8-14 AMP
*"The precepts of the Lord are right, **rejoicing the heart**; the commandment of the Lord*

*is pure and bright, **enlightening the eyes**. The [reverent] fear of the Lord is clean, enduring forever; the ordinances of the Lord are true and righteous altogether. More to be desired are they than gold, even than much fine gold; they are sweeter also than honey and drippings from the honeycomb. Moreover, **by them is Your servant warned (reminded, illuminated, and instructed); and in keeping them there is great reward. Who can discern his lapses and errors? Clear me from hidden [and conscious] faults. Keep back Your servant also from presumptuous sins; let them not have dominion over me!** Then shall I be blameless, and I shall be innocent and clear of great transgression. **Let the words of my mouth and the meditations of my heart be acceptable in Your sight**, O Lord, my [firm, impenetrable] Rock and my Redeemer."*

This passage denotes at the very least a conscious determination on our part, as a faith quality decision, to seek a divine remedy for our carnal tragedy! This passage is an acknowledgement that individually speaking: any man who agrees with the Word of God's Righteousness and Truth shall eradicate his iniquities from his wounded heart!

*You see, the Holy Spirit will give to us
the unfolding Word of His grace thereby allowing us
to unfold our past and the iniquities associated! Truly, Almighty
God has a remedy for man's carnal tragedy! Hallelujah!!!*

Because the traditional church has become dysfunctional in their impenitence, it is no wonder that spiritual leadership and especially pastors across the board refuse to embrace the teachings of repentance as they simply don't want to be told what to do! *For them, repentance has become a curse!* They remain the choke point for the rest of the corporate church! *They prefer their income, their position, possession and piety in place of the truth of Scripture with regards to iniquities, theirs as well as others.*

Lamentations 2:14 AMPC states,
"*Your prophets have predicted for you falsehood and delusion and foolish things; and **they have not exposed your iniquity** and guilt to avert your captivity [**by causing you to repent**]. But they have divined and declared to you false and deceptive prophecies, worthless and misleading.*"

Psalms 107:17 AMPC
*"Some are fools [made ill] because of the way of their transgressions and are **afflicted because of their iniquities.**"*

I must afflict my soul with repentance because my iniquities have afflicted my heart! Another way to consider this scenario is to assault my carnality with the salt of God's righteousness. In doing so, I violate my iniquities because I render experiential Truth as a judgment to the area of these lies. This also denotes that repentance is that which requires my involvement, *for a lifestyle of repentance is also my atonement as well as my affliction* for my iniquities, which remain as being unatoned for sin! *(cf. Le 23:27-29)*

My secret heart denotes a promiscuous and defiled conscience. Proverbs 14:10 states, the heart knows its own bitterness and no stranger shares its joy. This means that within the heart of every man God has placed a moral compass of sorts that directs him towards those things of God and those things that are normal and are not deviate. However, because iniquities abound, the heart becomes corrupted, abnormal and defiled. When a wounded heart becomes encased in this shell of carnality, the individual conceals his iniquities within—from himself. This is a case scenario of a state of denial, which in and of itself is an attribute of *lie-based thinking*!

Proverbs 5:22-23 AMPC
*"His own **iniquities shall ensnare** the wicked man, and he shall be held with the cords of his sin. He will die for **lack of discipline and instruction,** and in the greatness of his folly he will go astray and be lost."*

My iniquities are to me as a booby trap. ***This explosive device possesses the elements of deception that consists of the grenade of my carnality!*** And just as any booby trap will cause injury or death when triggered, so likewise does the explosive components, which is my iniquity, cause me to be ensnared, even trapped and cornered in the mind-field of my unatoned Lie-Based Thinking! Moreover, it will require a spiritual discipline of a lifestyle of repentance to avert, avoid and allay this iniquity from ever becoming a problem to begin with.

Isaiah 1:4a, c, 5b, 6b AMPC
*"Ah, sinful nation, **a people loaded with iniquity,** offspring of evildoers…they have despised and shown contempt and **provoked** the Holy One of Israel…The **whole head is sick,** and the **whole heart is faint** (feeble, sick and nauseated)…but **wounds***

*and bruises and fresh bleeding stripes; they have not been bound up or softened with oil [**No one has troubled to seek a remedy.**]"*

It is obvious that we must take the time and trouble to seek out a remedy for my carnal tragedy! Scripture tells us that *it is the glory of God to conceal a thing, but it is the honor of kings to search the matter* (of our iniquity) *out.* Question: *How can anyone come to know, understand and acknowledge his iniquity unless he searches the matter of his iniquity out?* He can't! It is for this reason why the Apostle Paul stated: *there is none righteous no not one.* There is none that understands! Understand what? Answer: The matter of our iniquity!

Jeremiah 3:13 AMPC
*"Only know, **understand** and **acknowledge your iniquity** and guilt—that you have rebelled and transgressed against the Lord your God and have scattered your favors among strangers under every green tree, and **you have not obeyed My voice**, says the Lord." (cf. Le 16:21-22; Ps 32:5)*

Isaiah 22:14 AMPC
*"And the Lord of hosts revealed Himself in my ears [as He said], surely this **unatoned sin** (iniquity) shall not be purged from you until [you are punished—and the punishment will be] death, says the Lord God of hosts."*

No wonder this world is going to hell in a hand basket! *Everyone alive is loaded with an innumerable multitude of iniquities!* The reason we live in a *world of iniquity* is do to this fact! The *whole head is sick!* This ailing health has caused the wounds of our hearts! *No wonder our hearts do fail and leave us feeling forsaken! These iniquities remain as unatoned sin because they are that which resides secretly within our deceived hearts! This iniquity is unatoned sin because the precious blood of Christ will not cover that which we don't uncover!* This is evident because of our fallen countenance.

Proverbs 25:2-5 AMP
*"It is the glory of God to conceal a thing, but the glory of kings is to search out the thing [so concealed]. As the heavens for height and the earth for depth, so the hearts and minds of kings are unsearchable. **Take away the dross from the silver, and there shall come forth [the material for] a vessel** for the silversmith [to work up]. **Take away the wicked from before the king, and his throne will be established in righteousness** (moral and spiritual rectitude in every area and relation)."*

Within each and every man there does exist a pure vessel. Consider a gold ring. In time, it becomes tarnished. So to remove the tarnish, you must apply a rubbing compound to restore its sheen. Is this not true? In like fashion, when we allow the Holy Ghost to take away the iniquities within our wounded hearts, we immediately become a righteous vessel of glory and honor to Almighty God! This spiritual patina will occur only as we are willing to allow the Holy Ghost to rub (even to our dislike) that which He knows must be done.

Isaiah 5:18 AMPC
*"Woe to those who draw [calamity] with **cords of iniquity** and falsehood, who bring punishment to themselves with a **cart rope of wickedness**."*

This *cart rope* in my mind denotes a *thick rope* spun specifically for pulling a heavy laden cart. This implies that an impenitent man employs the use of a thick rope that is fastened to his wounded heart and noosed *around his neck*! He in effect becomes a beast of burden for he is yoked to his iniquities!

This iniquity is unatoned sin because the precious blood of Christ will not cover that which we don't uncover!

Proverbs 5:22 AMPC
*"His own iniquities shall ensnare the wicked man, and he shall be held with the **cords of his sin**."*

Isaiah 6:7 AMPC
*"And with it he touched my **mouth** and said, Behold, this has touched your **lips**; your **iniquity** and guilt, are **taken away**, and **your sin is completely atoned for and forgiven**."*

Job 15:5 AMPC
*"For your **iniquity teaches your mouth**, and you choose the tongue of the crafty."*

Psalms 141:3-4 AMPC
"Set a guard, O Lord, before my mouth; keep watch at the door of my lips. Incline my heart not to submit or consent to any evil thing or to be occupied in deeds of wickedness with men who work iniquity; and let me not eat of their dainties."

Question: Why is iniquity often associated with the mouth, lips and tongue? Because iniquity is a heart issue, as a treasure, and whatever is within a wounded heart the mouth speaks! Scripture teaches that a man's *iniquity teaches his mouth* and when he speaks out this evil treasure within his defiled heart, he chooses the tongue that is a *world of iniquity*! *(cf. Isa 57:17; Mt 12:34-37; Jas 3:5-6)*

Furthermore, David acknowledged in *Psalms 141* that *he [was] is no different than any other man for he too has iniquity within his heart as well!*

Daniel 9:24…states, in the 70 weeks of years or 490 years, among other things, are decreed for the purpose of *the reconciliation of iniquity*. This then does not contradict *Isaiah 22:14*. But it does denote a prophecy pertaining to the New Testament Covenant through Jesus Christ who was *bruised for our iniquities*! By the word *reconciliation*, Scripture means that what was once unatoned for is now atoned or covered *so long as a man is willing to uncover his iniquity by coming to repentance. What is Iniquity?* It is that which is unatoned (covered) for. And since iniquity must be punished, Almighty God states that *physical death is the punishment for iniquity* just as Jesus Christ died for the sins of man! Furthermore, a lifestyle of repentance is the means whereby we uncover our falsehoods!

Typically, the anticipation of Jesus' second coming is regarded as the rapture, when all the saints of God shall be called home. By the time of the tribulation, *those who have died in the Lord* shall be raised from their graves, while *those who are still alive in the Lord* shall be changed in a twinkling of an eye, and altogether everyone shall be caught up in the air, having left this unrighteous world behind. *(cf. 1 Th 4:15-17)* What I get out of this text passage however is this; should mankind come to repentance and live righteously, living a godly life, Jesus Christ will delay His appearing as Judge of the Universe, allowing even additional time for the Gospel of the Kingdom to seep into the wounded hearts of sinful man! But alas, because impenitent men have condemned themselves to their own devices, their eventual demise evinces that they will not come to repentance, as Scripture does attest! They fail to realize their own iniquities have become the source of their own self-fulfilling prophecy!

Humanity fails to realize that *a lifestyle of repentance shall delay or postpone the "Or Else" consequences of an impenitent life. Conversely, unatoned iniquity shall become for the impenitent, his self-fulfilling prophecy, and not to his liking!* Jesus Christ shall return quickly, sooner not later, because of the corruption of carnal humanity. His return shall be based upon the past precedent of Genesis, in which Almighty God destroyed all living creatures from the face of the earth, and what He has done once; He shall most certainly do again!

Isaiah 27:9 AMPC
*"Only on **this condition shall the iniquity** of Jacob (Israel) **be forgiven and purged**,
and this shall be the **full fruit** [God requires], for **taking away his sin**: that [Israel]
should **make all the stones** of the [idol] altars **like chalk stones crushed to pieces**,
so that Asherim and the sun-images shall not remain standing or rise again."*
(cf. Isa 53:11; Mt 21:42-44)

*Coming to repentance is the only condition through which iniquity shall be purged and
forgiven!* In doing so, Almighty God receives the *full fruit* as the harvest of a converted
soul whose heart has been regenerated one lie at a time and one memory at a time. The
full fruit shall be the *fruition of His dividends* that we give back to God because of His
investment He has deposited within penitent men! Furthermore, *we should not leave
any stone of iniquity unturned! (cf. Eze 11:19)* This speaks of *one iniquity after another!*
The ultimate goal being that Almighty God would have a cultivated vineyard as *the
complete regeneration of a fully converted soul!*

Isaiah 30:13 AMPC
*"Therefore **this iniquity and guilt will be to you like a broken section of a high
wall, bulging out and ready [at some distant day] to fall**, whose crash will [then]
come suddenly and swiftly, in an instant."*

Luke 13:4-5 AMPC
*"Or those eighteen on whom **the tower in Siloam fell and killed them**—do you
think that they were more guilty offenders (debtors) than all others who dwelt in
Jerusalem? I tell you, No; but **unless you repent (change your mind for the better
and heartily amend your ways, with abhorrence of your past sins), you will all
likewise perish and be lost eternally."*

Presently, as of this writing, there is a section of Jerusalem's perimeter wall (southern
and eastern) that is sporting a very noticeable bulge. This therefore seems to be a fulfillment of this prophetic statement in that it also represents the iniquity of Israel as well
as the iniquity within the church! *(cf. La 2:18)*

This verse in *Isaiah 30* is also interesting to me because it speaks of a high wall that bulges out and that is ready to fall. Suppose this wall is a mason block wall that consists of

several courses or rows of mason block that eventually rises to a predetermined height. According to *Isaiah 30:13*, this wall is high, perhaps very high. Now suppose that this wall is joined at the corners to other walls of equal height. What you end up with is a fortress or blockade of sorts. Now depending on whether you are inside these walls or near the wall that bulges out would determine impending danger to you personally because of your iniquity. Here Scripture provides a description by way of an association made about the nature and character of iniquity. *Specifically that iniquity, due to its ability to multiply and to be innumerable has the capacity to overwhelm a man so much so that he is actually pent up (shut in or confined) in his iniquity from all sides.*

> *Romans 11:32 ISV*
> *"For God has locked all people in the prison of their own disobedience (iniquity) so that He may mercy on them all."*

Typically, a man will convince himself that he has all things in control. He will become confident in this and live his life with an air of arrogance until something unplanned for appears. Then, he is reminded that he really does not have control as he supposed. Eventually, he might come to realize that *control is just an illusion* that feeds on his vanity.

Like a lava tube deep beneath the surface that is filled with hot molten lava. It eventually will erupt through a volcano. Man's iniquity is like lava that is constantly flowing within the deep recesses of the mind and heart waiting to erupt here and there and do so without notice. It is at the ready to explode due to the implosion of a wounded heart! As Scripture implies, so long as man remains impenitent, he is ignorant of his future end. *(e.g., De 32:28-29, 36)* And speaking of remains, *just as a cadaver is unconscious to the things in life, so too then is any man willfully ignorant who chooses to remain in his iniquity, for he is unconscious to the things of God!*

> *Isaiah 32:6 AMPC*
> *"For the fool speaks folly and **his mind plans iniquity: practicing profane ungodliness and speaking error concerning the Lord, leaving the craving of the hungry unsatisfied and causing the drink of the thirsty to fail.**" (cf. Job 13:23; Ps 64: 5-6)*

Iniquity is planned for within the spirit of the mind (all 4 quadrants). *It is for this reason why the mind is carnal!* Scripture teaches that Almighty God can cause us to know our iniquities; but we must be willing and courageous to allow ourselves to confront these heart issues and permit the Holy Ghost access to eradicate them with His Truth!

Isaiah 53:11a, d AMPC
*"He shall see [the fruit] of the travail of His soul and be satisfied…for **He shall bear the iniquities** and their guilt [with the consequences, says the Lord]." (cf. Isa 27:9)*

The *full fruit* pertains to *the bearing of the multitude of iniquities, like a fully fruited tree!* This particular verse especially shall remain as another Scripture verse whose truth has yet to be experienced in the area of experiential knowledge. *Whereas, Jesus Christ did bear our iniquities, so to then must we come to know, understand and acknowledge them for ourselves!* As we do so, then we too shall become a fully fruited tree of righteousness in the Spirit. But if we choose not to know, understand and acknowledge our iniquities, then we shall bear them alone and they shall become as that evidence used against us in court (the Bema Seat). However, since we choose to acknowledge them and judge them via repentance, then we keep the charge of the sanctuary! *(cf. Isa 27:9; Jer 3:13)*

*Zechariah 3:7 [*Adam Clarke Commentary]*
"If thou wilt walk in my ways—If ye, Israelites, priests and people, now restored to your own land, will walk in my ways, etc. ye shall be a part of my family and have [places-mansions- in eternal glory, with all them that are sanctified."

Job 13:26-27 AMPC
*"For You write bitter things against me [**in Your bill of indictment**] and make me inherit and be **accountable now for the iniquities of my youth.** You put my feet **also in the stocks and observe critically all my paths**; You set a circle and limit around the soles of my feet [which I must not overstep]." (cf. Job 14:7; Isa 59:2-4, 12-13)*

This indictment is a formal accusation of a serious crime that is presented by a grand jury. It is also a statement of indictment that *something is wrong (iniquity) for there is somebody (humanity) to blame. In this sense our iniquities become the source of our condemnation for they are a reflection of our stony heart!*

As an indictment, our iniquity is also a charge which is levied against us for having violated God's Law! Furthermore, this indictment is a court summons for prosecution! The *stocks* speak of a penalty that must be paid, for *any impenitent man has violated the probation period of his living.* Therefore, Almighty God watches us with His critical eye in hopes man would acknowledge there is nothing about him that is not observed and known by his Cre-

---

*Clarke, Adam. "Commentary on Zechariah 3:7". "The Adam Clarke Commentary" https://www.studylight.org/commentaries/acc/zechariah-3.html. 1832. Public domain.

ator! My iniquities are the unatoned sins still residing within my soul. *It is these that shall be used as evidence against me on the day of my reckoning so long as I remain impenitent.*

Jeremiah 14:7 KJV
*"O Lord, though our **iniquities testify against us**, do thou it for thy name's sake: for our backslidings are many; we have sinned against thee."*

Isaiah 64:6c-7 AMPC
*"...we all fade like a leaf, and **our iniquities, like the wind**, take us away [far from God's favor, hurrying us towards destruction]. And **no one calls on Your name and awakens and bestirs himself to take and keep hold of You**; for You have hidden Your face from us and have delivered us into the [consuming] **power of our iniquities**." (cf. Jer 5:25; Isa 59:2-4)*

Like a backfire that is started to quench a raging forest fire, Almighty God is a consuming fire, whose fire shall overpower the power of my iniquities! And like fire brands that are carried in the wind ahead of a raging wildfire, so likewise are my iniquities the lies and deception that are blown about in the wind of deceit within the vast theater of my mind. Scripture tells us that God's Judgment shall fall to the earth like leaves that fall from vines and trees. Our iniquities then are the fuel for the fire of God's judgment!

⚷

They fail to realize their own iniquities have become the source of their own self-fulfilling prophecy!

Isaiah 34:4 KJV
*"And all the host of heaven shall be dissolved, and the heavens shall be rolled together as a scroll: and all their hosts shall fall down, as **the leaf that falleth off from the vine, and as a falling fig from the fig tree**."*

Isaiah 57:19 AMPC
*"Peace, peace to him who is afar off [both Jew and Gentile] and to him who is near! says the Lord. **I create the fruit of his lips**, and I will heal him [**make his lips blossom anew with speech in thankful praise**]."*

Question: *How does God create the fruit of my lips?* When I allow His Holy Spirit to shine His Divine Truth (experientially) upon my iniquity (lie - based thinking)! *Remember that iniquity is the lie - based thinking that is the treasure of a wounded heart.*

The following passages describe wounds as those injuries inflicted by another and the reason why. *(Note verses 4, 7, 13 and 15)*

Isaiah 59:1-18 AMPC

59 1 *"Behold, the Lord's hand is not shortened that it cannot save, nor His ear dull with deafness, that it cannot hear.*

2 **But your iniquities have made a separation between you and your God, and your sins have hidden His face from you, so that He will not hear.**

3 **For your hands are defiled with blood and your fingers with iniquity; your lips have spoken lies, your tongue mutters wickedness.**

4 *None sues or calls in righteousness [but* **for the sake of doing injury to others**—*to take some undue advantage];* **no one goes to law honestly** *and pleads [his case] in truth; they trust in emptiness, worthlessness and futility, and* **speaking lies!** *They* **conceive mischief and bring forth evil!**

5 *They hatch* **adder's eggs** *and weave* **spider's web***; he who eats of their eggs dies, and [from an egg] which is crushed a viper breaks out [for their nature is ruinous, deadly, evil].*

6 *Their webs will not serve as clothing, nor will they cover themselves with what they make; their works are* **works of iniquity** *and the act of violence is in their hands.*

7 *Their feet run to evil, and they make haste to shed innocent blood. Their* **thoughts** *are* **thoughts of iniquity***; desolation and destruction are in their paths and highways.*

8 *The way of peace they know not, and there is no justice or right in their goings. (cf. Ro 3:17) They have made them into crooked paths; whoever goes in them* **does not know peace.**

9 *Therefore are justice and right far from us, and righteousness and salvation do not overtake us. We expectantly wait for light, but [only]* **see darkness***; for brightness, but* **we walk in obscurity and gloom.**

10 *We grope for the wall like the blind, yes; we* **grope like those who have no eyes.** *We* **stumble at noonday** *as in the twilight; in dark places and among those who are full of life and vigor, we are as dead men.*

11 *We all groan and growl like bears and moan plaintively like doves. We look for justice, but there is none; for salvation, but it is far from us.*

12 *For our transgressions are multiplied before You [O Lord], and* **our sins (iniquity) testify against us***; for our transgressions are with us, and* **as for our iniquities,**

we know and recognize them [as]:

13 Rebelling against and denying the Lord, turning away from following our God, speaking oppression and revolt, conceiving in and muttering and moaning <u>from hearts words of falsehood</u>.

14 Justice is turned away backward, and righteousness and right standing with (God) stands far off; for truth has fallen in the street (the city's forum), and uprightness cannot enter [the courts of justice].

15 Yes, truth is lacking, and he who departs from evil makes himself a prey. And the Lord saw it, and it displeased Him that there was no justice.

*16 And He saw that there was no man and wondered that there was no intercessor [**no one to intervene on behalf of truth and right**]; therefore His own arm brought Him victory, and His own righteousness [having the Spirit without measure] sustained Him.*

17 For [the Lord] put on righteousness as a breastplate or coat of mail, and salvation as a helmet upon His head; He put on garments of vengeance for clothing and was clad with zeal [and furious divine jealousy] as a cloak.

18 (According as their deeds deserve, so will He repay wrath to His adversaries, recompense to His enemies; on the foreign islands and coastlands He will make compensation)." (cf. Isa 34:8, 33:24)

Revelations 21:27 AMPC
"But nothing that defiles or profanes or is unwashed shall ever enter it, nor anyone who commits abominations (unclean, detestable, morally repugnant things) or <u>practices falsehood</u>, but only those whose names are recorded in the Lamb's Book of Life."

Jeremiah 2:6-7 AMPC
*"Nor did they say, where is the Lord, Who brought us up out of the land of Egypt, who led us through **the wilderness**, through **a land of deserts and pits**, through **a land of drought and of the shadow of death** and **deep darkness**, through **a land that no man passes through**, and **where no man dwells**? And I brought you into a plenteous land to enjoy its fruits and good things…"*

There is a place in God known as *there*! This place is also known as *God's Country*. This land is not terra firma, but it is a place nonetheless. It is that place where Almighty God dwells in Truth, Justice and Righteousness and it is reserved for the righteous—those who have come to this place and time in their lives where their iniquities are known, understood and acknowledged for what they really are, unatoned sin aka: falsehoods!

Jeremiah 3:2a, 2d-4 AMPC
*"...where have you not been adulterously lain with? ...and **you have polluted the land with your vile harlotry and your wickedness**...Yet you have **the brow of a prostitute;** you refuse to be ashamed. Have you not just now cried to Me; My Father, **You were the guide and companion of my youth?**"*

No doubt that any prostitute often ponders the innocence of her youth. But due to her lie-based thinking (iniquity) she continues to do wickedly, thereby practicing her falsehoods. How she must long for the days of yesteryear, when she was innocent—so it is with all men. We ponder the former days and our innocent ways of our youth whenever we are pressed and compassed by our turbulent present. Would to God that all men would come to *know, understand and acknowledge* their iniquities that Almighty God might forgive us of our wickedness! *We must all know that the goodness of God leads us to repentance. (cf. Ro 2:4)*

Jeremiah 3:13 AMPC
*"Only **know, understand** and **acknowledge your iniquity** and guilt—that you have rebelled and transgressed against the Lord your God and have scattered your favors among strangers under every green tree, and **you have not obeyed My voice, says the Lord."** (cf. Ps 32:5; Le 16:21-22)*

Iniquity has attached its lies to memories and thus, God's Truth must target these wounds as I *unfold them,* lie after lie, and memory after memory. In doing so, I come to know, understand and acknowledge my iniquity. *To confess all my iniquities will require my entire lifetime. This then provides the reason and the purpose for a lifestyle of repentance!* By placing myself on the altar of God, daily taking up my cross I identify with the crucifixion of Christ.

Jeremiah 9:6 AMPC
*"**Your habitation is in the midst of deceit [oppression upon oppression and deceit upon deceit]; through deceit they refuse to know and understand Me,** says the Lord."* (cf. Ro 3:10-11, 17)

Iniquity is an *imagined reality* and habitation as a place of residence. What's more, it is a house of bondage in which terror and torment does exist and thrive. But this Scripture states that *Almighty God also dwells in the midst of the deceit caused by our iniquities and oppression.* He is not the cause, but He is the remedy to this carnal tragedy! In other words, He abides in His Truth and Almighty God would have us to know that He is waiting there for us individually if we would only allow ourselves to go there!

Psalms 90:8 AMPC
*"Our iniquities, **our secret heart** and its sins [**which we would so like to conceal even from ourselves**], You have set in the [revealing] light of Your countenance."*

Jeremiah 16:17 AMPC
*For My eyes are **on all their ways; they are not hidden from My face, neither is their iniquity concealed from My eyes.**" (cf. La 4:22)*

My iniquity resides behind a cognitive veil. (See Fig. 7, p. 83) This veil is that which either separates or divides the conscious from the subconscious where iniquity resides within the spirit of my mind. It is for this reason why I must come to know, understand and acknowledge my own iniquity because that is precisely where Almighty God dwells—where His truth is intended to be. In fact, Almighty God is stating that (He knows us better than we know ourselves!)

Jeremiah 30:14d-15b AMPC
*"...**because your sins (iniquity) are glaring and innumerable. ..Because of the greatness of your perversity and guilt because your sins are glaring and innumerable, I have done these things to you.**"*

Iniquity can be accumulated. It can exist in clusters like grapes on a vine. If you consider the vine to be a memory and the cluster, the lies attached to it, then you can picture the impact of these verses.

Military weaponry includes among many other things explosive devices known as *cluster bombs.* These devices have the capability to inflict injury, death and destruction to multiple targets at a time. *So it is with the accumulation of iniquities. They become cluster devices of traumatic, tradition or demonic origins that target several areas of a wounded heart!* However, just as a cluster bomb is an explosive device before it is deployed against a target, so likewise is there a *predominant iniquity* that is also as an explosive device that causes multiple reactions. When the predominant iniquity is targeted with God's Truth, the other associated cluster lies often times are also destroyed at the same time!

Lamentations 2:14 AMPC
*"**Your prophets have predicted for you falsehood and delusion and foolish things; and they have not exposed your iniquity and guilt to avert your captivity [by causing you to repent]. But they have divined and declared to you false and de-***

ceptive prophecies, worthless and misleading."

A true prophet of God will expose iniquitous thoughts thereby causing one to come to repentance! For it is only through repentance that the truth and the light of God's Word will gain access to our iniquity. Unfortunately, existing spiritual leadership (pastors) are reluctant to open their pulpits to a genuine prophet of God. But this is nothing new since Scripture contains several examples of those leaders as well as Israel itself in antiquity whom chose not to heed the message of the prophet of God! Consider the following passages.

⌐

Would to God that all men would come to know, understand and acknowledge their iniquities that Almighty God might forgive us of our wickedness!

Isaiah 3:1-4 AMPC
"For, behold, the Lord, the Lord of hosts, is taking away from Jerusalem and from Judah the stay and the staff [every kind of prop], the whole stay of bread and the whole stay of water, the mighty man and the man of war, the judge and the [professional] prophet, the one who foretells by divination and the old man, the captain of fifty and the man of rank, the counselor and the expert craftsman and the skillful enchanter. And I will make boys their princes, and with childishness shall they rule over them [with outrage instead of justice]."

Job 12:24 AMPC
***He takes away understanding from the leaders** of the people of the land and of the earth, and causes them to wander in a wilderness where there is no path."*

Ezekiel 12:2-4 AMPC
*"Son of man, **you dwell in the midst of the house of the rebellious,** who have eyes to see and see not, who have ears to hear and hear not, for **they are a rebellious house.** Therefore, son of man, **prepare your belongings for removing and going into exile,** and move out by day in their sight; and you shall remove your place to another place in their sight. It may be they will consider and perceive that they are a rebellious house. And you shall bring forth your baggage by day in their sight, as*

baggage for removing into exile; and you shall go forth yourself at evening in their sight, as those who go forth into exile."

Matthew 23:37-39 AMPC
*"O Jerusalem, Jerusalem, murdering **the prophets and stoning those who are sent to you!** How often would I have gathered your children together as a mother fowl gathers her brood under her wings, **and you refused! Behold, your house is forsaken and desolate** (abandoned and left destitute of God's help). For I declare to you, you will not see Me again until you say, Blessed (magnified in worship, adored and exalted) is He who comes in the name of the Lord!"*

Lamentations 4:12-13 AMPC
*"The **kings of the earth did not believe, nor did any of the inhabitants of the earth,** that the oppressor and enemy could enter the gates of Jerusalem. **[But this happened] because of the sins of her [false] prophets and the iniquities of her priests, who shed the blood of the just and righteous** in the midst of her."*

Lamentations 2:14 AMPC
*"Your **prophets have predicted for you falsehood and delusion and foolish things;** and they have **not exposed your iniquity** and guilt **to avert your captivity [by causing you to repent]**. But they have divined and declared to you false and deceptive prophecies, worthless and misleading."*

How is it that the blood of the just and the righteous are shed? *It is shed when the watchman fails to warn of impending destruction.* His neglect is the same as not keeping the charge of the sanctuary. As a result, the blood of the just and righteous, even the innocents is shed—*all because of neglect.* Consequently, their blood shall be required at the watchman's hand! *(e.g., Eze 33:1-9)*

Ezekiel 7:19c AMPC
*"…they shall not satisfy **their animal cravings** nor fill their stomachs with them, for [wealth] has been **the stumbling block of their iniquity**." (cf. Eze 44:12)*

Iniquity is also a stumbling block. It is that which causes one to stumble, trip, fall, stub your toe. It is that which is a carnal booby-trap that is designed to cripple thereby impeding or retarding any spiritual victory. *(e.g., 1 Ti 1:9-10)*

1 Timothy 1:5b AMPC
"*...who **imagine that godliness or righteousness is a source of profit** [a money-making business, a means of livelihood]. **From such withdraw.**"*

Ezekiel 24:23 AMPC
"*And your turbans shall be upon your heads and your shoes upon your feet; you shall not mourn or weep, but **you shall pine away for your iniquities...**"*

Have you ever noticed the emaciated appearance of people whose countenance conveys subliminal messages, without their conscious awareness and leaving you with the notion of pity? Their countenance has fallen because of their iniquities! They literally pine (sulk, brood, pout) away in them because they have become ensnared by their lie-based thinking! Their countenance evinces a fallen look. Their eyes have that 2000 yard stare similar to those who have been in an extended battle front. This is also very evident when you gaze into their eyes, for our eyes are the windows to their soul. This fallen condition also is seen amongst nations and their citizens who are duped by an aberrant ideology such as the radical Muslim or Communism. They have pined away sulking and this is evident because in their minds, America and Israel are the root cause of all their problems!

Ezekiel 28:18 AMPC
"*You **have profaned your sanctuaries by the multitude of your iniquities** and the enormity of your guilt, **by the unrighteousness of your trade.** Therefore I have brought forth **a fire from your midst...**"*

What I like about this verse is that *commerce shall be targeted by a corrective fire from within* its midst. I suspect that the *world's stock markets shall be consumed from within* causing a worldwide economic collapse and all because of the greed and the fear that motivates or forces oppression across all societies. This also coincides with the mega-churches and prominent ministries whose bottom line supports the opulent lifestyle of their respective leaders. Although these *Christian businesses* do employ hundreds, and perhaps thousands, according to Scripture, these institutions of commerce shall also be as fuel for the fire of God and *all because of the multitude of iniquities*!

Since I am the house of God and the dwelling place of the Holy Ghost, *then I must seek righteous judgment during these days of my probation against the iniquities that still reside within my heart!* This is a gradual process of purging. I only have the rest of my natural life to accomplish this. *My life and all the days I have left, are the ongoing and continuous days of repentance towards the conversion of my soul via the renewing of the spirit of my mind.*

Ezekiel 32:27 AMPC
*"And they shall not lie with the mighty who have fallen of the uncircumcised [and] who have gone down to Sheol (the place of the dead, the netherworld) with their weapons of war, whose swords were laid [with honors] under their heads and **whose iniquities are upon their bones, for they caused their terror to spread in the land of the living.**"*

Iniquity is unatoned falsehood. It is so because iniquity is that which has yet to be confessed and eradicated from within the wounded heart. This Scripture infers that *there is a definite health risk and that to our skeletal frame!* Whereas, Jeremiah said that *he had God's fire shut up in his bones, (cf. Jer 20:9)* this verse implies that *the fire of hell caused by our iniquity shall exist within our bones!* Furthermore, Jeremiah also states that a man becomes *a terror to himself and to society* because of his unatoned iniquity! Furthermore, Jesus Christ even stated that the corporate church is tainted with this soulful pathogen of iniquity!

Would to God that all men would come to know, understand and acknowledge their iniquities that Almighty God might forgive us of our wickedness!

Matthew 23:27-28 KJV
*"Woe unto you, scribes and pharisees, hypocrits! For ye are like unto whited sepulchres which indeed appear beautiful outward, but are within full of **dead men's bones** and of all uncleanness. Even so, ye also outwardly appear righteous unto men, but within ye are full of hypocrisy and iniquity."*

Jeremiah 20:3-6 AMPC
*"And the next day Pashur brought Jeremiah out of the stocks. Then Jeremiah said to him, The Lord does not call your name Pashur, but Magor-missabib [terror on every side]. For thus says the Lord; Behold, I will make you **a terror to yourself and to your friends**; they will fall by the sword of their enemies while you look on. And I will give all Judah into the hand of the king of Babylon and will slay them with the sword....and you Pashur, and all who dwell in your house shall go into captivity; you shall go to Babylon, and there you shall die and be buried, you and all your friends to whom you have prophesied falsely."*

Here again, Scripture speaks of the sword and previously we learned that a *scepter is considered to be the Sword of State. When a man chooses to live his life in his iniquities, then that man shall die beneath the Sword of State of his own falsehoods!* He fails to realize that life as a whole for everyone is all about authority! We can choose to live our life in authority over or we may choose to live out our life under or beneath the authority of another! What's more, his influence upon others will cause them to also die in like fashion, unless of course each person comes to a lifestyle of repentance.

Psalms 125:3 AMPC
*"For **the scepter of iniquity** shall not rest upon the land of the [uncompromisingly] righteous, lest [unless] the righteous (God's people) stretch forth their hands to iniquity and apostasy."*

→ The Unfolding of the Cognitive Veil ←

Psalms 32:5 AMPC
*"I acknowledge my sin to You, and **my iniquity I did not hide**. I said, I will confess my transgressions to the Lord [**continually unfolding the past till all is told**]— then You [instantly] forgave me the guilt and iniquity of my sin. Selah [pause, and calmly think of that]!*

Psalms 119:130 AMPC
*"The entrance and **unfolding of Your words** give light; **their unfolding** gives understanding (discernment and comprehension) to the simple."*

In the following passages below and as a review, see whether you can discover for yourselves each *type of lie* and every *category or classification of iniquity*. As you do so, ask the Holy Spirit to give you the Spirit of Wisdom and Revelation in the knowledge of Him with the understanding that He resides in truth and that His truth must exist or extend through the cognitive veil of your mind and into its subconscious arena. These iniquitous lies are *types that explain their function*. In fact, just as there are 7 categories of iniquity, so also there are 8 types of lies, they are: *Metamorphic, Cluster, Clone, Memory-linked, Guardian, Splinter, Osmotic and Thematic*. Furthermore, these lies are also *categorized according to their nature and character*. There are 8 categories, they are: *Fear Lies, Abandonment Lies, Shame Lies, Tainted Lies, Hopelessness Lies, Invalidation Lies, Powerlessness Lies and Confusion Lies.*

2 Corinthians 4:3-6 AMPC
*"But even if our Gospel (the glad tidings) also **be hidden (obscured and covered up with a veil that hinders** the knowledge of God), it **is hidden** [only] **to those who are perishing and obscured** [only] **to those who are spiritually dying and veiled** [only] **to those who are lost.** For the god of this world **has blinded the unbeliever's minds** [that they should not discern the truth], **preventing them from seeing the illuminating light of the Gospel** of the glory of Christ (the Messiah), Who is the Image and Likeness of God…For God Who said, Let light shine out of darkness, **has shone in our [wounded] hearts,** so as [to beam forth] the Light for the illumination of the knowledge of the majesty and glory of God [**as it is manifest in the Person and is revealed**] **in the face of Jesus Christ** (the Messiah)."*

Isaiah 59:2 AMPC
*"But your iniquities have made a **separation between you** and your God, and your sins have **hidden His face from you,** so that He will not hear."*

Question: Could it be that the iniquity of man is or has become [as it were] the god of this world?

Now, the word *cognitive relates to thought processes and to the mental processing of acquired knowledge by the use of reasoning, intuition or perception.* (Encarta Dictionary) However, as pertaining to the expression the *Knowledge of God, Daath Elohim,* (Hebrew Translation) *cognitive* is also defined as *personal involvement, emotional attachment and inner commitment.* Now it seems that man's iniquities, as our hidden unatoned sin, are the very thing which divides, and separates us from God! In fact, comparing Scripture with Scripture, it appears that man's iniquity provides every indication (evidence and character) of *the god of this world.*

Psalms 19:8-14 AMP
*"The precepts of the Lord are right, **rejoicing the heart**; the commandment of the Lord is pure and bright, **enlightening the eyes.** The [reverent] fear of the Lord is clean, enduring forever; the ordinances of the Lord are true and righteous altogether. More to be desired are they than gold, even than much fine gold; they are sweeter also than honey and drippings from the honeycomb. Moreover, by them is Your servant warned (reminded, illuminated, and instructed); and in keeping them there is great reward. Who can discern his lapses and errors? **Clear me from hidden [and conscious] faults. Keep back Your servant also from presumptuous sins; let them not have dominion***

*over me! Then shall I be blameless, and I shall be innocent and clear of great trans-gression. **Let the words of my mouth and the meditations of my heart be acceptable in Your sight**, O Lord, my [firm, impenetrable] Rock and my Redeemer."*

In the above passages, I find a correlation of this cognitive veil. Specifically that *this veil is that which separates or divides. (See Fig. 7)* The vertical centerline (head) represents the cognitive veil that exists to hinder, obscure or otherwise separate the light *and the knowledge of Truth of God from entering the area of our wounded heart wherein resides the iniquities.* Now, when you think of wounds, are they not often accompanied with emotional pain? Occasionally, the emotional pain is so traumatic that it causes a circuit overload to our conscious mind. Since *the mind is designed of God in such a way to survive,* it automatically will position an emotional event *to great to retain* in the conscious behind the cognitive veil and into the subconscious realm. *It is here in the subconscious that present emotional pain manifests itself although the accurate memory was a reflection of a past event.*

(Figure 7)

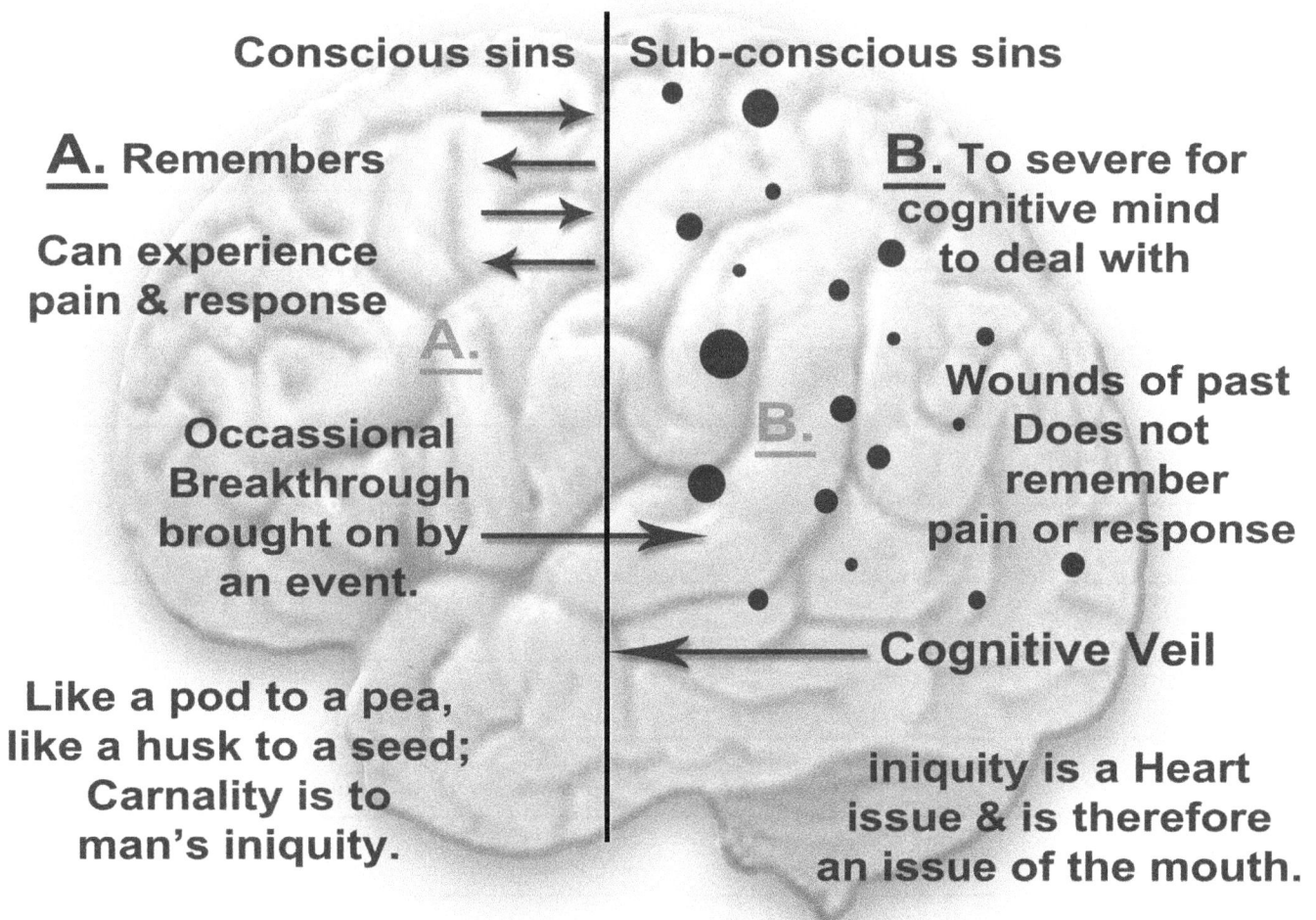

Conscious sins | Sub-conscious sins

A. Remembers

Can experience pain & response

A.

B. To severe for cognitive mind to deal with

Wounds of past Does not remember pain or response

Occassional Breakthrough brought on by an event.

B.

Cognitive Veil

Like a pod to a pea, like a husk to a seed; Carnality is to man's iniquity.

iniquity is a Heart issue & is therefore an issue of the mouth.

(Mt 12:34-37; Isa 6:7)

⚷

Now it seems that man's iniquities, as our hidden unatoned sin, are the very thing which divides, and separates us from God!

The smaller circles in the head denote iniquities (lie-based thinking, deception, delusions, false hoods) contained in our memories caused by stab or puncture wounds. These perforations represent the injuries and trauma endured, encountered and experienced in life that are to severe (over load) for the cognitive mind to deal with or process consciously. Hence, these memories with the attached iniquities become lodged in the subconscious realm where they remain as misinterpreted rationality and imagined reality, and this is because the memory association is either visual (sensory), emotional, physical or a combination thereof.

[Feel free to research the Scripture passages I have already referenced in the margin of this sketch. It is hot off the Holy Ghost Press!]

Notes:_____

_____

_____

_____

_____

_____

_____

_____

_____

_____

_____

Notes:_____

Notes:

Section 5

→ The god(s) of this World ←

2 Corinthians 4:3-4 AMPC

*"But even if our Gospel (the glad tidings) also be hidden (obscured and covered up with a veil that hinders the knowledge of God), it is hidden [only] to those who are perishing and obscured [only] to those who are spiritually dying and veiled [only] to those who are lost. For **the god of this world** has blinded the unbelievers' minds [that they should not discern the truth], **preventing them from seeing** the illuminating light of the Gospel of the glory of Christ (the Messiah), Who is **the Image and Likeness of God.**"*

Isaiah 59:2 AMPC (Parentheses mine)

*"But your **iniquities** (Lie - Based Thinking) **have made a separation** between you and your God, and your sins have **hidden His face** from you, so that He will not hear."*

1 John 4:3 AMPC

"And every spirit [word] which does not acknowledge and confess that Jesus Christ has come in the flesh [but would annul, destroy, sever, disunite Him]. This [non-confession] is the [spirit] of the antichrist, [of] which you heard that it was coming, and now is already in the world."

Hebrews 1:2-3 AMPC

"[But] in the last of these days He has spoken to us in [the person of a] Son, Whom He appointed Heir and lawful Owner of all things, also by and through Whom He created the worlds and the reaches of space and the ages of time [He made, produced, built, operated, and arranged them in order]. He is the sole expression of the glory of God [the Light-being, the out-raying or radiance of the divine], and He is the perfect imprint and the very image of [God's] nature, upholding and maintaining and guiding and propelling the universe by His mighty power..."

While editing, I was impressed to make a connection between *2 Corinthians 4:3-4* and *Isaiah 59:2*. And the question that I had was, *Could it be that the iniquity of man is the key indicator as the spirit of antichrist belonging to the god of this world?* In other words, is our iniquity antiChrist? I ask this since both passages denote that God's face (Image and Likeness) is hidden from impenitent men.

I am reminded of a parenting life style. No matter if the parents are a good, wholesome and loving influence, or they are not, when they pass on, the influence that is left behind in their grown children remains. And because of this, the children will perpetuate that parental influence onto their children and society as a whole.

Well, based upon *Ezekiel 28:16-19* the influence of this fallen and expired Guardian Angel has remained throughout the history of humanity. Could it be then that the iniquity and carnality of man is the ongoing influence of this entity?

Iniquity: Defined: Hebrews Reference #5753: *A-vah* means: to crook, lit or fig. –do amiss, bow down, make crooked, commit iniquity, pervert, (do) perversely, do wickedly, do wrong, trouble, to overthrow. Ref #5771: *avon* means: (moral) evil:--fault, iniquity, mischief, punishment (of iniquity), sin.

Iniquity: Defined: Greek Reference #458: *anomia* means: illegality, i.e. violation of law or (gen) wickedness—iniquity, transgression of law, *unrighteousness*. Ref. #459 *anomos* means: lawless, not subject to the law, wicked:--without law, lawless, transgressor, unlawful, wicked.

The other thought that came to mind was the Scripture verse that speaks of *the god of the belly. (cf. Php 3:19)* as well as the verses that state that *we are gods. (e.g., Ps 82:6, Joh 10:34-35)*

It's been said that *a spade is a spade* and that *if it sounds like a duck, if it looks like a duck—it's probably a duck!* These euphemisms are used to convey a more neutral, vague or indirect expression of a potentially more offensive, harsh or unpleasant term. And this is significant since I am about to expose a theological mind set as to *who* or *what* this god *potentially* is!

But before I do, let me share this thought. In the movie '*300*' the Persian King was portrayed as a 7 foot tall, opulently dressed heathen man. He repeatedly said that he was a merciful god to all whom he spoke with. Do you remember? Although this was a 2007 movie, I find it very fascinating that Scripture has a very similar if not exact historical event as well! This event is found in *Ezekiel 28*, specifically, in the first 19 verses. So I copied these passages from the Bible to show you here.

⛏

Could it be then that the iniquity and carnality of man is the ongoing influence of this entity?

As I read the first 19 verses, I immediately could see a comparison. This comparison involves the imagined reality of the King of Tyre and his lie - based thinking (his iniquity) as resembling the activities of an *angelic guardian* who fell out of grace and fellowship with Almighty God. *(Of interest are verses 16-19).* These passages tell us the demise of this angelic guardian. Gee, I wonder if this was—Satan? If so, then Almighty God consumed him in fire in front of all those standing by. And since this is a true account, how is it then that Lucifer, Satan or the Devil has so much fanfare?

A Message for Tyre's King

28 *1 Then this message came to me from the LORD:*

2 "Son of man, give the prince of Tyre this message from the Sovereign LORD: "In your great pride you claim, 'I am a god! I sit on a divine throne in the heart of the sea.' But you are only a man and not a god, though you boast that you are a god.

3 You regard yourself as wiser than Daniel and think no secret is hidden from you.

4 With your wisdom and understanding you have amassed great wealth—gold and silver for your treasuries.

5 Yes, your wisdom has made you very rich, and your riches have made you very proud.

6 "Therefore, this is what the Sovereign LORD says: Because you think you are as wise as a god,

7 I will now bring against you a foreign army, the terror of the nations. They will draw their swords against your marvelous wisdom and defile your splendor!

8 They will bring you down to the pit, and you will die in the heart of the sea, pierced with many wounds.

9 Will you then boast, 'I am a god!' to those who kill you? To them you will be no god but merely a man!

10 You will die like an outcast at the hands of foreigners. I, the Sovereign LORD, have spoken!"

11 Then this further message came to me from the LORD:

12 "Son of man, sing this funeral song for the king of Tyre. Give him this message from the Sovereign LORD: "You were the model of perfection, full of wisdom and exquisite in beauty.

13 You were in Eden, the garden of God. Your clothing was adorned with every precious stone—red carnelian, pale-green peridot, white moonstone, blue-green beryl, onyx, green jasper, blue lapis lazuli, turquoise, and emerald—all beautifully crafted for you and set in the finest gold. They were given to you on the day you were created.

14 I ordained and anointed you as the mighty angelic guardian. You had access to the holy mountain of God and walked among the stones of fire.

15 "You were blameless in all you did from the day you were created until the day evil was found in you.

16 Your rich commerce led you to violence, and you sinned. So I banished you in disgrace from the mountain of God. I expelled you, O mighty guardian, from your place among the stones of fire.

17 Your heart was filled with pride because of all your beauty. Your wisdom was corrupted by your love of splendor. So I threw you to the ground and exposed you to the curious gaze of kings.

18 You defiled your sanctuaries with your many sins and your dishonest trade. So I brought fire out from within you, and it consumed you. I reduced you to ashes on the ground in the sight of all who were watching.

19 All who knew you are appalled at your fate. You have come to a terrible end, and you will exist no more."

Scripture teaches that Almighty God is God above all other gods, and to this I wholeheartedly agree! But Scripture does speak of *the god of this world*. So my attempt in this investigative report/segue will be to ascertain just what is this god and who is he/it? Again, I shall answer the basic investigative questions of Who, What, When, Where, Why and How.

To begin with all things of the spirit are intangible, whether those things are of God or not. When you think of an emotion such as love or joy for example, can you see it? What does it love look like? For that matter, can anyone ever provide a physical description of any emotion? Of course not; but what can be provided is a mannerism. So with just an indication to begin with, the god of this world *may be described solely upon the basis of its characteristics or mannerisms that pertain to its influence upon men and our conduct and behavior towards it.* In essence, you could say that its manner is as a smoke trail which when traced back to its place of origin, the fire of hell itself shall be found!

Who is the god of this world? My traditional or religious guess tells me that the *god of this world* is none other than *Satan* himself. But who is this Satan and what is it? *Could it be that what is commonly or traditionally considered as Satan is nothing more than corporate vain imaginations of antiquity or mythology by the religious elite and by those who have made bad choices in and throughout their lives and because of their choices life's circumstances became adversarial to them!* Of interest to me is that my KJV Bible states that Lucifer in *Isaiah 14:12* was identified as the king of Babylon *but that the church world has erroneously taught, thought and believe this is a reference to Satan.* For me this admonishment is an important key. Primarily, because this teaching is incorrect!!! In *Revelations 1:18*, Jesus Christ is stating that He alone has the *keys of hell and of death* and that in *Revelations 9:1*, we read that the fifth angel *was given the key to the bottomless pit.*

Below I extracted a fascinating report from the internet about (a man) the king of Babylon, Lucifer and the idolatrous man king Ahaz who was the ruler over Judah in *Isaiah 7 through 14.*

Is "Lucifer" the Devil in Isaiah 14:12?
The KJV Argument against Modern Translations

The argument that modern translations deny the deity of Christ is based on connecting several dots. First, In Isaiah 14:12 in the KJV we read: *"How art thou fallen from heaven, O Lucifer, son of the morning! how art thou cut down to the ground, which didst weaken the nations!"* Modern translations—except for the NKJV—have something like "day star" or "morning star" instead of "Lucifer" here. KJV advocates claim that *Isaiah 14:12* must be a prophecy about the devil falling from Heaven. There is some basis for this interpretation.

In *Luke 10:18* Jesus tells his disciples, *"I saw Satan fall like lightning from heaven."* In *Revelations 9:1 ESV* we read, *"I saw a star fallen from heaven to earth, and he was given the key to the shaft of the bottomless pit".*

▪ 1. These New Testament passages seem to be alluding to *Isaiah 14:12*, connecting the fall of the one mentioned there with the fall of Satan.

▪ 2. In *2 Peter 1:19* the KJV has: *"We have also a more sure word of prophecy; whereunto ye do well that ye take heed, as unto a light that shineth in a dark place, until the day dawn, and the day star arise in your hearts."* For *"day star"* in the KJV, modern translations alternate between 'day star' and 'morning star.' Early Christian interpretation of this verse sees the 'day star' or 'morning star' as a reference to Jesus, based in part on an allusion to *Numbers 24:17* ("*A star shall rise out of Jacob*").

■ **3.** KJV advocates argue that if the word in *Isaiah 14:12* is translated 'morning star' then modern translations are viewing Jesus as Satan because, as they claim, the only 'morning star' in the Bible is Jesus. Thus, if 'Lucifer' is treated as 'morning star' in *Isaiah 14:12*, then this is a denial of the deity of Christ.

■ **4.** They argue that God is not a God of confusion and therefore the modern translations, since they are confusing readers on the identification of the morning star, must be corrupt.

To be frank, this is a rather convoluted argument that is grasping at straws. An examination of the evidence and logic of this argument will demonstrate it to be very badly misinformed.

In *Isaiah 14:12, The KJV translators did not actually translate the Hebrew word* לליהֹ *as* '*Lucifer.*' This word occurs only here in the Hebrew Old Testament. Most likely, the KJV translators *were not sure what to make of it, and simply duplicated the word used in the Latin Vulgate translated* לליהֹ. In the Vulgate, *Isaiah 14:12* reads as follows:

> *quomodo cecidisti de caelo lucifer qui mane oriebaris corruisti in terram qui vulnerabas gentes.*

Notice the fifth word of the text—*lucifer*. It is not a proper name but the Latin word for 'morning star.' The word *Lucifer* occurs four times in the Vulgate: *Isaiah 14:12, Job 11:17, Job 38:32,* and *2 Pe 1:19.* In *Job 11:17,* the KJV renders the Hebrew word רקֶבֹ as 'morning':

> *et quasi meridianus fulgor consurget tibi ad vesperam et cum te consumptum putaveris orieris ut lucifer*

In *Job 38:32*, the KJV renders the Hebrew word תורזמֹ as Mazzaroth. This is another word that occurs only once in the Hebrew Bible. *The KJV translators did not know what it meant, so they simply transliterated the Hebrew into English characters.* Even though Jerome, the translator of the Vulgate, knew Hebrew better than the KJV translators did, he was not exactly sure what to make of it either. But he at least tried, rather than simply leave the word untranslated as the KJV translators did. He translated the word as *lucifer*—or 'morning star,' which is very close to the meaning of the Hebrew תורזמֹ:

numquid producis luciferum in tempore suo et vesperum super filios terrae consurgere facis

The word means 'constellations' or 'crowns' (modern translators are not sure, though 'constellations' is usually preferred). The fact that Jerome recognized that at least the תורזמ probably referred to stars is far better than the KJV translators did by leaving the word completely untranslated. There is of course no conspiracy on Jerome's part here; he is simply being faithful to the Hebrew Bible and is translating as accurately as he can.

In *2 Peter 1:19*, the KJV renders the Greek word φωσφόρος (*phosphoros*) as 'day star.' Again, the Latin Vulgate has *Lucifer* here:

et habemus firmiorem propheticum sermonem cui bene facitis adtendentes quasi lucernae lucenti in caliginoso loco donec dies inlucescat et <u>lucifer</u> oriatur in cordibus vestris

In other words, *lucifer* is not a proper name, but is the Latin word for 'morning star' or 'day star.' The KJV simply reproduced the Latin in *Isaiah 14:12 because they were not sure what* לליה *meant.*

The KJV translators knew Latin better than they knew Greek or Hebrew. In places where they were not sure what the Greek or Hebrew meant, they simply translated or reproduced verbatim the Latin text. This has happened scores, if not hundreds, of times.

Since that time, *Lucifer* has made its way into English Bible interpretation as another name for the devil. If there is a conspiracy to sabotage the deity of Christ by translating the Hebrew word לליה in *Isaiah 14:12* as 'morning star,' the same as is done with φωσφόρος in *2 Peter 1:19*, then this conspiracy goes back to Jerome at the beginning of the fifth century AD! In reality, he translated the Hebrew word faithfully and the Greek word faithfully.

It is the KJV that did not translate the word at all, but rather retained the Latin rendering of Jerome in *Isaiah 14:12* and worse, simply transliterated the Hebrew in *Job 38:32*. Also Jerome cannot be charged with not knowing Hebrew well. He moved to Bethlehem and lived there for 35 years while he worked on the translation. He wanted to learn Hebrew well; making his home for 35 years in the land of the Jews is sufficient proof of that.

But aren't the references to the individuals in *Isaiah 14:12* and *2 Peter 1:19* as the morning star in modern translations confusing? And thus don't modern translations undermine the deity of Christ?

The reality is that in *Isaiah 14:12* the primary or initial reference of 'morning star' is not to the devil but to the Babylonian king. The footnote in the NET Bible here says, *"What is the background for the imagery in verses 12–15?* This whole section *(vs 4b–21)* is directed to the king of Babylon, who is clearly depicted as a human ruler. Other kings of the earth address him in *(v 9)*, he is then called 'the man' in *(v 16)*, and, according to *(vs 19–20)*, he possesses a physical body."

⚷

> ### *When one examines the evidence with an open mind, many modern translations are seen to be clearer and closer to the original text than the KJV is.*

At the same time, *Isaiah 14:12–15* seems to go beyond a description of a mortal king. Further, if Jesus in *Luke 10:18* and John in *Revelations 9:1* had this passage in mind, then it is evident that there is a secondary meaning that relates to the devil himself. A double-fulfillment prophecy is thus probably in view.

Here's the point: if the primary referent is to the Babylonian king (which the great majority of biblical scholars would affirm and as the evidence mentioned in the NET Bible footnote lists), then our understanding of the use of 'morning star' in *2 Peter 1:19* makes sense. The morning star literally referred to Venus, but in ancient times it was used metaphorically of earthly kings. The note in the NET Bible at *2 Peter 1:19* is helpful along these lines:

The reference to *the morning star* constitutes a double entendre. First, the term was normally used to refer to Venus. But the author of course has a metaphorical meaning in mind, as is obvious from the place where the morning star is to rise— "in your hearts."

Most commentators see an allusion to *Numbers 24:17* ("a star shall rise out of Jacob") in Peter's words. Early Christian exegesis saw in that passage a prophecy about Christ's coming. Hence, in this verse Peter tells his audience to heed the OT Scriptures which predict the return of Christ, then alludes to one of the passages that does this very thing, all the while running the theme of light on a parallel track. In addition, it may be significant that Peter's choice of terms here is not the same as is found in the LXX. He has used a Hellenistic word that was sometimes used of emperors and deities, perhaps as a further polemic against the paganism of his day.

In other words, 'morning star' or *lucifer* in the Latin Vulgate literally referred to Venus, but metaphorically would refer to earthly kings, emperors, and pagan deities. Peter thus may have chosen this word to show that the real morning star was Jesus, not Caesar. *Isaiah 14:12* thus spoke of the Babylonian king as the morning star and predicted his fall. Jesus and John used this text to indicate that Satan would fall.

It is only by turning *lucifer* into a proper name, as has been done by KJV advocates, that misunderstanding of the meaning of these texts could occur. The logic of the KJV position is as follows:

Lucifer is a proper name and refers exclusively to one who is inherently evil, the devil. Thus, even if translated as 'morning star' in *Isaiah 14.12*, this still refers exclusively to the devil. Consequently, for Jesus to be called 'morning star' in *2 Peter 1:19* is to call him the devil.

The logic breaks down on the first premise, viz., that the term in *Isaiah 14:12* refers exclusively to one who is evil. Since this is false, the conclusion is also false. To call Jesus 'morning star' in *2 Peter 1:19* makes him no more evil than calling Satan 'god' (*cf. 2 Co 4:4*) makes him good. And to argue that since God is not the God of confusion and therefore different words must be used in each verse is to continue to compound the false view of *lucifer*—as a name for the devil.

It is an illegitimate hermeneutic to claim that because the term in one place refers to one person, therefore the same term in another place must be to the same person. There are scores of examples of a term used in the Bible as referring primarily to one thing/person, but having a different thing/person in view if the context demands it. As hinted above, 'God' is used primarily of the one true God of the Bible, but there are occasional references in which *human beings (e.g., Joh 10:34–35)* or *Satan (e.g., 2 Co 4:4)* are called 'god'—even in the KJV.

Further, if pressed, the argument actually backfires on <u>KJV only</u> advocates. For example, the Name 'Jesus' is the Greek form of the Hebrew name Joshua. In the New Testament, there are three references to Joshua. On two of these occasions, the KJV translators translated the name as 'Jesus.' But in each instance this rendering is misleading, in the second case badly so.

Acts 7:45 KJV
*"Which also our fathers that came after brought in with **Jesus** into the possession of the Gentiles, whom God drave out before the face of our fathers, unto the days of David"*

Acts 7:45 NET
*"Our ancestors received possession of it and brought it in with **Joshua** when they dispossessed the nations that God drove out before our ancestors, until the time of David."*

The context is clearly about Joshua and the Hebrews going into the promised land and conquering the nations there. Why the KJV has 'Jesus' here is a mystery to me. Perhaps they were trying to be literal here (by transliterating the Greek word *Iesous* as 'Jesus'), but if so why did they not do this in *Luke 3:29*, where Jesus' genealogy is enumerated (and *Iesous*, an ancestor of Jesus, is rendered 'Jose')?

Far more troublesome is *Hebrews 4:8 KJV*
*"For if **Jesus** had given them rest, then would he not afterward have spoken of another day."*

NET (New English Translation)
"For if Joshua had given them rest, God would not have spoken afterward about another day."

Again, the context is *somewhat* clear that Joshua is in view. But to the reader who is not paying careful attention to the context and who does not know that "Jesus" here is really *Joshua*, he could easily be misled into thinking that Jesus Christ was not able to give His people rest. As such, this could certainly undercut the deity of Christ—especially in light of *Hebrews 4:3 NET* which says, *"As I swore in my anger, 'They will never enter my rest!'"*

Further, since a proper name is used each time (unlike *Isaiah 14:12* and *2 Peter 1:19*), it would be much harder for the average reader to distinguish which Jesus is being talked about. The argument that God is not a God of confusion certainly applies much more to the KJV than to modern translations in this instance.

Does this mean that the KJV is wrong at this place? Technically no. But in terms of clarity to the average reader, it can be very confusing. At bottom, those who argue that the KJV is the only Holy Bible are using flimsy arguments that turn on themselves. And this reveals the real reason why they don't care for modern translations: it is an issue of emotional attachment.

When one examines the evidence with an open mind, many modern translations are seen to be clearer and closer to the original text than the KJV is. The KJV is still an important translation for English-speaking Christians to own and read. It is the single greatest literary monument to the English language ever produced by a committee. Its lyrical quality, cadence, memorable phrases that linger in the mind, and elegance make it a translation that has stood the test of time. Some modern translations rival it on these attributes (especially the ESV, REB, and NET), and they are far more accurate as well. These should be the primary Bibles that English-speaking Christians read, but neither they nor the King James have an *exclusive claim to the throne.

★ [This exegetical study was written by Daniel B. Wallace PH.D. from Dallas Theological Seminary.]

According to Scripture then, the name Lucifer was a title given to (a man) king of Babylon for he stood as an adversary to Judah in *Isaiah 14*. In fact, as I read this chapter from verse 4 a proverb was spoken against the (man) king of Babylon! *According to the Strong's Exhaustive Concordance, the defining characteristics of Satan have everything to do with the derivatives of one's conduct and behavior, which also embraces their heart motivations.* I find it very interesting that the devil or Satan is mentioned just a handful of times in Scripture. For example: in *Leviticus 17:7* and *2 Chronicles 11:15* we read that the Hebrews offered up sacrifices to devils, even in the high places. According to the Strong's Concordance, (#8163) the word *devils* means a shaggy he-goat or by analysis a fawn, goat, hairy, kid, rough, satyr. In other words, this animal (through no fault of its own) had been tagged as a representation of Satan or the devil!

In *Deuteronomy 32:17*, we read that they sacrificed unto devils... the word *devils* is defined to mean a *daemon* (a [person's] attendant spirit; a demon) or as a *person* who is or

---

*It is important to note that the KJV translators did as good a job as could be expected in the early seventeenth century. Our criticism here is not of the KJV translation but of KJV advocates who have canonized the translation as though it were the only Holy Bible.

that which is malignant (hateful, spiteful, mean, nasty, wicked, cruel). Do you know any-one who might fit this description? As a cross reference, the Strong's identifies #7736 to mean to swell up by implication of insolence.

Again, this does not specifically identify a devil/Satan as a spirit god! *What it does por-tray is a person's conduct and behavior that seemingly emerges from a defiled conscience (Heart)!* And yet the concordance does not specifically define Satan or the devil to be the *adversarial spirit god*!

Finally, the only other Old Testament reference is found in *Psalms 106:37*. In this verse, sons and daughters were offered up to devils. Sounds like wholesale murder to me and *the people themselves chose to abort the lives of their own children*! Just recently, the country of Iceland claimed Down syndrome in infants has been dealt with. They report that Down syndrome no longer exists in Iceland because of abortions!

Once again, the Strong's Concordance defines these devils to be *the act of malignancy. In other words, with regards to one's character, conduct and behavior, action etc.* So keep-ing all things in context, if there were a devil it is the individual and not some imagi-nary spirit god.

So, with this revelation fresh in your mind, to be fair what does Almighty God have to say about Himself—that is, His God-self?

> *In Dueteronomy 4:35 Almighty God declares that the Lord,* **He is God; there is none else besides Him...**

> *Deuteronomy 32:39a KJV*
> *"See now that **I, even I am He, and there is no god with me.**"*

> *2 Samuel 7:22 KJV*
> *"Wherefore thou art great, O Lord God: for there is none like thee, **neither is there any God beside thee**, according to all that we have heard with our ears."*

> *1 Chronicles 17:20 KJV*
> *"O Lord God: for there is none like thee, **neither is there any God beside thee**, ac-cording to all that we have heard with our ears."*

Psalms 83:18 KJV
*"That men may know that thou, whose name is Jehovah, **art the most high over all the earth**."*

Psalms 86:10c KJV
*"...**thou art God alone**."*

Isaiah 43:10-12 KJV
*"Ye are My witnesses, saith the Lord, and My servant whom I have chosen; that ye may know and believe Me, **and understand that I Am He: before Me there was no God formed, neither shall there be after Me, I, even I am the Lord; and beside Me there is no savior**. I have declared, and have saved, and I have shewed when there was **no strange god among you**; therefore ye are My witnesses, saith the Lord, that I Am God."*

Just as there is a *Throne of Iniquity* which bears the *Scepter of Iniquity,* Man's own malignant heart sits upon its own throne of deceptive stratagems and these *sponsoring thoughts* wields their Scepter with the authority to manipulate individuals and nations who remain unaware of the influences of their own defiled consciences upon and within their very lives!

Although this misinterpreted Satan cannot be seen physically as something material, its influence may be perceived. This is also true with the Spirit of Almighty God. His Holy Spirit cannot be seen, however this does not negate His existence! *In a way, the ambiance of the god of this world presides as an atmosphere over the affairs of all impenitent men, like a global conscience!* Conversely, the Spirit of God presides over the affairs of all of His people, specifically, but also when all is said and done, His Authority shall reign supreme, even over that of a Satan. *So the answer to this question is that the god of this world is a spirit, and since man was created in the image and likeness of Creator God as spirits, it stands to reason that men are the gods of this world!*

▪ ***What is the god of this world?*** According to Scripture, it is a deceiving *spirit word* that blinds the minds of all unbelievers from seeing the Light of the Gospel of the glory of Christ, Who is the Image and the Likeness of God. This perceived god is also that which hides God's face from us. It is the spirit of antichrist that is sponsored by a base thought of irresponsibility. *(cf. 1 Joh 4:3)*

▪ ***What makes Satan the god of this world?*** So long as men *refuse to forgive* others of their offenses against them and as long as *impenitent men choose* to ignore Heaven's provision for wounded hearts and emotional pain, then by or through default, Satan [their defiled conscience] assumes the throne as the god of their unrighteous world, which each man creates for him or herself. This in turn makes impenitent men the gods of this world and that of their own choosing!

⚷

... the Spirit of God presides over the affairs of all of His people, specifically, but also when all is said and done, His Authority shall reign supreme, even over that of a Satan.

▪ *When does the god of this world exist?* It is common knowledge that *you may kill a man, but you cannot kill a spirit, for any spirit is eternal.* Therefore, the god of this world is an eternal spirit that inhabits history and since man's existence is a temporal occupation in the annals of infinity, the god of this world also exists seemingly as an unintended event.

▪ *Where does the god of this world exist?* Scripture speaks of the **heavens* such as the Kingdom of Heaven and the Kingdom of God and the *Heaven of heavens*. It's been said that all things are parallel--*That which is spirit is manifested in the material and vice versa.* Since there does exist *heavenly realms* such as the atmosphere of earth, the stratosphere, as that realm between the atmosphere and outer space, and just as there are the *various kingdoms* that do exist simultaneously such as the *animal kingdom* that coexists with the *insect kingdom* and the *kingdom of man* which coexists with the *plant kingdom*, and the *kingdom of Self*, etc, it is not difficult to understand and accept the validity of the existence of heavens. Since man was created as a spirit creature, all things that pertain to him are also spirit in form, function and facility spiritually. By this I mean too say that although his spirit resides in a physical dirt body and he has a soul, the truth of the matter is that even that which is physical is in reality invisible. This has been confirmed at the microscopic level for under extreme levels of magnification, any object that exists may be shown to consist of molecules that are unseen to the naked eye! Herein, is found another *kingdom of the molecular*! It is known as nanotechnology!

Now the brain is a physical organ of the anatomy. You can see it and operate on it. The

---

*The NET here has 'sky' for 'heaven,' with the following note: "Or 'from Heaven' (the same Greek word means both 'heaven' and 'sky')."

brain may be removed from a skull and preserved. It is no different with the computer. The computer is a solid object and has weight. It is designed in many different ways and for so many more different applications and facilities. The computer has the capacity for cyberspace as that area wherein imagery is provided for any computer user. *What cyberspace is to the computer's capacity for imagery, the brain has the capacity for what is known as the spirit of the mind!*

It is the mind that enables man to project images within the theater of his imagination. This then would qualify the mind to be spirit as well. This also applies to the minds of all unbelievers and since it is a spirit, the god of this world resides within this spirit realm also. What's more, because humanity has its origins from the dirt, these deceptions prefer to reside in the dirt of Humanity!

- *Why does the god of this world exist?* According to the traditional theology Scripture teaches that Lucifer, the anointed Cherub, attempted to usurp Almighty God. Jesus Christ stated that He saw Satan fall to earth as a bolt of lighting. Ever since, Satan and his deceiving spirits roam in dry arid places looking for rest. They search for rest because to their thinking or purpose usurping Almighty God indirectly is better than the direct approach that failed! *But there is another reason why the god of this world exists.* Perhaps I should restate it another way. *Perhaps the god of this world proliferates due to the impenitence men!*

- *How does the god of this world exist?* The god of this world lives within the hearts and minds of all men whose hearts have been wounded. The proof of this existence is found in all lie-based thinking that is attached to our wounded hearts and memories.

Whereas, a wound is that injury that was inflicted by another generally, *the god of this world is a wound to the heart of God caused by man's impenitence* and its proliferation by all men who refuse to know the truth! Why? *Because all of humanity have become practitioners of our own falsehoods!* Just as presently, the nations of this world are very concerned about the nuclear proliferation among certain hostile nations, so likewise is Almighty God very concerned about the *increase* of iniquity within the hearts of all men.

Revelations 21:27 AMPC
"But nothing that defiles or profanes or is unwashed shall ever enter it, nor anyone who commits abominations (unclean, detestable, morally repugnant things) or practices falsehood, but only those whose names are recorded in the Lamb's Book of Life."

➔ Whatever You say to this Mountain ⬅

Mark 11:22-26 AMP

*"Truly I tell you, whoever says to this mountain, Be lifted up and thrown into the sea! And **does not doubt at all in his heart but believes that what he says** will take place, it will be done for him. For this reason I am telling you, whatever you ask for in prayer, **believe** (trust and be confident) that it is granted to you, and you will [get it]. And whenever you stand praying, if you have anything against anyone, **forgive him** and let it drop (leave it, let it go), in order that your Father Who is in heaven may also **forgive you** your [own] failings and short comings and let them drop. **But if you do not forgive, neither will your Father in heaven forgive your failings and shortcomings.**"*

How many times have I heard teachings on this passage, from a preacher whose message fails to go beyond the norm? Sensing that there was always something missing or over looked; I knew that I would have to wait upon the Holy Ghost *to unfold deeper truths* that in my opinion have been overlooked. Typically, it is often heard that all one must do is say to the mountain, and do not doubt. But should the truth be told, it is a common dilemma for most that *what they may speak (cognitively, logically) is contrary to that which they truly believe!* And I apply this towards the lie-based thinking that resides within the darkest recesses of the subconscious. In other words, whatever lie that exist in a specific area of our subconscious as a stronghold—say any addiction, the individual will display his true belief about himself in this area based upon a present event that triggers a remote memory. His belief would be founded upon what he feels within his wounded heart and not what he experiences. This feeling intuits his true belief, albeit a false belief at that! *Until our iniquities are exposed as the source of our lie - based thinking, then the spiritual benefits of this passage shall not be received!*

Isaiah 59:1-18 AMPC

*"Behold, the Lord's hand is not shortened that it cannot save, nor His ear dull with deafness, that it cannot hear. **But your iniquities have made a separation between you and your God,** and your sins have hidden His face from you, so that He will not hear. For your hands are defiled with blood and your fingers with iniquity; your lips have spoken lies, your tongue mutters wickedness. None sues or calls in righteousness [but for the sake of doing injury to others—to take some undue advantage]; no one goes to law honestly and pleads [his case] in truth; they trust in emptiness, worthlessness and futility, and **speaking lies!** They **conceive mischief and bring forth evil!** They hatch adder's eggs and weave spider's web; he who eats*

of their eggs dies, and [from an egg] which is crushed a viper breaks out [for their nature is ruinous, deadly, evil]. Their webs will not serve as clothing, nor will they cover themselves with what they make; their works are **works of iniquity** *and the act of violence is in their hands. Their feet run to evil, and they make haste to shed innocent blood. Their thoughts are* **thoughts of iniquity**; *desolation and destruction are in their paths and highways. The way of peace they know not, and there is no justice or right in their goings. They have made them into crooked paths; whoever goes in them does not know peace. Therefore are justice and right far from us, and righteousness and salvation do not overtake us. We expectantly wait for light, but [only] see darkness; for brightness, but we walk in obscurity and gloom. We grope for the wall like the blind, yes; we grope like those who have no eyes. We stumble at noonday as in the twilight; in dark places and among those who are full of life and vigor, we are as dead men. We all groan and growl like bears and moan plaintively like doves. We look for justice, but there is none; for salvation, but it is far from us. For our transgressions are multiplied before You [O Lord], and* **our sins (iniquity) testify against us**; *for our transgressions are with us, and as for our iniquities, we know and recognize them [as]: Rebelling against and denying the Lord, turning away from following our God, speaking oppression and revolt, conceiving in and muttering and moaning from hearts words of falsehood. Justice is turned away backward, and righteousness and right standing with (God) stands far off; for truth has fallen in the street (the city's forum), and uprightness cannot enter [the courts of justice]. Yes, truth is lacking, and he who departs from evil makes himself a prey. And the Lord saw it, and it displeased Him that there was no justice. And He saw that there was no man and wondered that there was no intercessor [no one to intervene on behalf of truth and right]; therefore His own arm brought Him victory, and His own righteousness [having the Spirit without measure] sustained Him. For [the Lord] put on righteousness as a breastplate or coat of mail, and salvation as a helmet upon His head; He put on garments of vengeance for clothing and was clad with zeal [and furious divine jealousy] as a cloak. According as their deeds deserve, so will He repay wrath to His adversaries, recompense to His enemies; on the foreign islands and coastlands He will make compensation."*

Because Scripture is not a book of actual illustrations, it does however contains literally thousands of spiritual associations so that you and I might picture in our minds the significance of spiritual truth—both logically as well experientially. For myself, because I am not a formally trained medical doctor or a scientist, it is always best when I can see the actual effects or results of spiritual consequences in the physical realm.

Below, I have obtained an item of interest that hopefully would breach the gap from that which is unknown (spiritual) to that which is known (tangible). So having studied this entire text hopefully you can appreciate *the authority of your iniquities* (lie-based thinking).

→ The Black Box and the Book of Conscience ←

The Flight Data Recorder (FDR) aka: the *Black Box* (which is actually red or orange) is first an electronic *monitoring device* which is installed in those computers aboard aircraft, submarines, ships, even the space shuttle. This device *records* all communications between pilots as well as all electronic data *for the life* of the aircraft, etc. This recorder is also found within the computer itself only it is known as a hard drive. Should an aircraft crash, for example, the National Transportation Safety Board and FAA investigators would retrieve this recorder for their investigative purposes at their lab and (purge) the information. This also means that should the aircraft be lost in the depths of the ocean, these agencies would dive to the depths of the seas to retrieve this vital data!

Even in criminal cases, the criminologist would gain access to the information contained in the computers hard drive as *evidence used either for or against a suspect so charged.* Both devices are electronic and therefore must be *stimulated* electronically to induce the *exposure* of the memory content. Access is obtained via *a negative and a positive charge* in an alternating current as this is the only possible manner to acquire this *cryptic* or forensic information. Once the investigators acquire this data, they are then able to decipher *or learn the causes* of a crash or *gain knowledge* of the personal habits of a criminal before the commission of a crime. In fact, I've read that Microsoft shall soon be installing Black Boxes in their newer computers to ascertain the reasons why their computers crash.

Did you know that Scripture contains illustrative passages, which describe a Black Box within man? And when you consider a Black Box as a *memory* device wherein all events are recorded over the life of an aircraft or the hard drive of a personal computer which contains the *history* of technical information throughout the life of the computer, in like manner Almighty God has installed a *Black Box/hard drive* within the heart of everyone! *Perhaps this is why people state that their whole life flashes before them when faced with certain death or near death experiences!*

This Black Box is the *conscience*, which is one of the four faculties of the spirit of the mind. Just as the monitoring device is electronic, so to then *does a man's conscience monitor, record, document and retain the entire history of the individual*, for Scripture tells us that the dead were judged (sentenced) by what they had done [their whole way of feeling and acting, their aims and endeavors] *in accordance with what was recorded in the books. (cf. Re 20:12)* This includes all our memories all lies associated to these memories as well as our performance in accordance to programming of our lie-based thinking! Now just as any electronic device must be plugged into the current, so likewise *should every man plug into faith*, specifically having faith in the blood of Christ, Jesus! This means also that any other pseudo faith even denominational faith is not intended! Once plugged in, the alternating current has a means to flow. Is this not so? And just as the Black Box is built into the aircraft and is part and parcel to the aircraft's avionics all monitoring processes continue through the black box having an entry and an exit, so far as the power charge is concerned.

In Scripture, a *book* is described as being either opened or closed. *(cf. Ex 17:14; Isa 30:8, 9; Da 12:4; Mal 3:16; Re 20:12)* And in each book, as there are references to several, certain explanations are written whether it would be for godly conduct and behavior, or not, or whether it be in references to war, etc. As pertaining to the *book of conscience* it is apparent that this *monitor device* actually records all memories (good and bad), all lies, all false perceptions, all and everything that you and I have ever experienced, discussed, encountered whether as an offense, traumatic situations, etc. This *Book of Conscience* is built into the framework of the spirit of our mind and is also part and parcel to all that we are individually. And just like the investigators who must electronically stimulate the device to gain access to the memory data, so also must our *book of conscience* be *spiritually stimulated* if Almighty God or we are to gain access to its memory content! Whereas, the alternating current consists of *a positive and negative charge* to induce the black box to reveal its memory content, so also there exist a *spiritual energy* that shall induce the *book of conscience* to reveal or *expose the iniquities and ulterior motives of our secret heart!* Only this spiritual charge is a mandate from God Himself and it consists of repentance and forgiveness! *Whereas, faith (in the Blood) is the plug in, forgiveness of offenses and repentance for iniquities is that spiritual alternating current! (See Fig. 8, p. 109)* The only negative side to this charge is the confrontation of our stuff, for it takes courage on our part to confront our falsehoods! *(cf. Lu 18:1)* After that, we would enjoy the healing of our emotional pain experientially as well as freedom from offenses! This is true revival!

Now *Isaiah 22:14* below states that the only punishment for iniquity is death! This death has everything to do with mortifying the deeds of the flesh. *(cf. Ro 8:13)* Almighty God has provided man two attributes of His amazing grace. *They are called repentance and forgiveness.* Whenever a man chooses to forgive others of their offenses against him and vice versa, then that man shall be set free of them. And so long as that man chooses to come to repentance as *atonement for his iniquity*, then that man shall become a useful and valuable vessel of honor (gold and silver) in service to Almighty God. However, should any man refuse to apply these two elements of God's grace to his heart, then he shall die in his iniquities and then shall he stand in the midst of the small and the great and shall be judged from the book of his own conscience for the impenitence of his heart! *Either way, death shall be the punishment for iniquity!* One is for the here and now as it pertains towards our iniquities unto our honor; and the other shall be the *second death unto eternal damnation!* You see? It all comes down to the real issues and motives of the heart. Consider the following:

What an electrode stimulus is to certain areas of the brain psychologically, iniquity is to the motivation of the heart's bondage within specific areas of memory!

⚷

Almighty God has installed a Black Box/hard drive within the heart of everyone! Perhaps this is why people state that their whole life flashes before them when faced with certain death or near death experiences!

What a *misinterpretation of a memory* is to lie-based thinking (iniquity), the re-run of iniquitous thoughts are to scratched records!

What a *black box* is to all recorded electronic data and communication of and within an aircraft (avionics), so likewise does the *Book of Conscience (black box) of a man record all memories of events within a his life* as well as *monitors* his every deed and thought in and throughout every day of his living!

Just as a *black box* is accessed by electronic stimulation to retrieve crucial data, so likewise is the *Book of Conscience* opened by a *certain divine electrical charge (forgiveness and repentance)* that unlocks the book and reveals the memory contents of a man's conscience!

What faith is to an electrical plug in, forgiveness and repentance are to the alternating current of a divine charge! *(cf. Zec 3:7; Ac 17:30)*

Isaiah 22:14 AMPC
"And the Lord of hosts revealed Himself in my ears [as He said], surely this unatoned sin (iniquity) shall not be purged from you until [you are punished—and the punishment will be death, says the Lord God of hosts."

2 Timothy 2:19-21 AMPC
"But the firm foundation of (paid by) God stands, sure and unshaken, bearing this seal (inscription): The Lord knows those who are His, and, let everyone who names [himself by] the name of the Lord **give up all iniquity** and stand aloof from it. But in a great house (you, me) there are not only vessels of gold and silver, but also [utensils] of wood and earthenware, and some for honorable and noble [use] and some for menial and ignoble [use]. So whoever cleanses himself [from what is ignoble and unclean, who separates himself from contact with **contaminating and corrupting influences (iniquity)**] will [then himself] be a vessel set apart and useful for honorable and noble purposes, consecrated and profitable to the Master, fit and ready for any good work." (Parentheses are mine).

Psalms 32:5 AMPC
"I acknowledge my sin to You, and my **iniquity I did not hide**. I said, I will confess my transgressions to the Lord [continually **unfolding the past till all is told**]—then You [instantly] forgave me the guilt and iniquity of my sin."

Psalms 119:130 AMPC
"The entrance and **unfolding of Your words** give light; **their unfolding** gives understanding (discernment and comprehension) to the simple.

Hebrews 9:14 AMPC
"How much more surely shall the blood of Christ, Who by virtue of [His] eternal Spirit [His own preexistent divine personality] has offered Himself as an unblemished sacrifice to God, **purify our consciences** from dead works and lifeless observances to serve the [ever] living God?"

Hebrews 9:14 (Paraphrased)
"How much more surely shall the blood of Christ, who by virtue of His eternal Spirit, purify our consciences from dead works and lifeless observances to serve the ever living God."

Hebrews 10:17 AMPC
"He then goes on to say, and their sins (iniquity) and their lawbreaking (transgressions) I will remember no more." (Parenthesis mine)

Revelations 20:12 AMPC
*"I [also] saw the dead, great and small; they stood before the throne, and books **(of conscience) were opened**. Then another Book was opened, which is [the Book] of Life. And the dead were judged (sentenced) by what they had done [their whole way of feeling and acting, their aims and endeavors] **in accordance with what was recorded in the books.**" (Parentheses mine)*

I can best explain all these deep insights illustratively, only remember that all this has everything to do with the issues of your heart. *(See Fig. 8, p. 109)*

➔ Father Hood and Our Self Opinions ⬅

Luke 1:16-17 AMP
*"And he will turn back and cause to return many of the sons of Israel to the Lord their God, and he will [himself] go before Him in the spirit and power of Elijah, to turn back the hearts of the fathers to the children, and the disobedient and incredulous and unpersuadable to **the wisdom of the upright** [which is the knowledge and the holy love of the will of God]—in order to make ready for the Lord a people [perfectly] prepared [in spirit, adjusted and disposed and placed in the right moral state]."*

Malachi 4:5-6 AMP
*"Behold, I will send you Elijah the prophet before the great and terrible day of the Lord comes. And he shall turn and reconcile the hearts of the [estranged] fathers to the [ungodly] children, and the hearts of the [rebellious] children to [the piety of] their fathers [**a reconciliation produced by repentance of the ungodly**], lest I come and smite the land with a curse and a ban of utter destruction."*

I suppose that the first place to begin would be with the heart of the father. Not only our heavenly Father's but mine as well. Is my heart reconciled with His? In other words, although I may honor my heavenly Father with my lips, if there is unatoned sin (iniquity) resident, then my heart is far from His! And should this be the case, my heart has failed me because it has been enlarged with a multitude of iniquities!

(Figure 8)

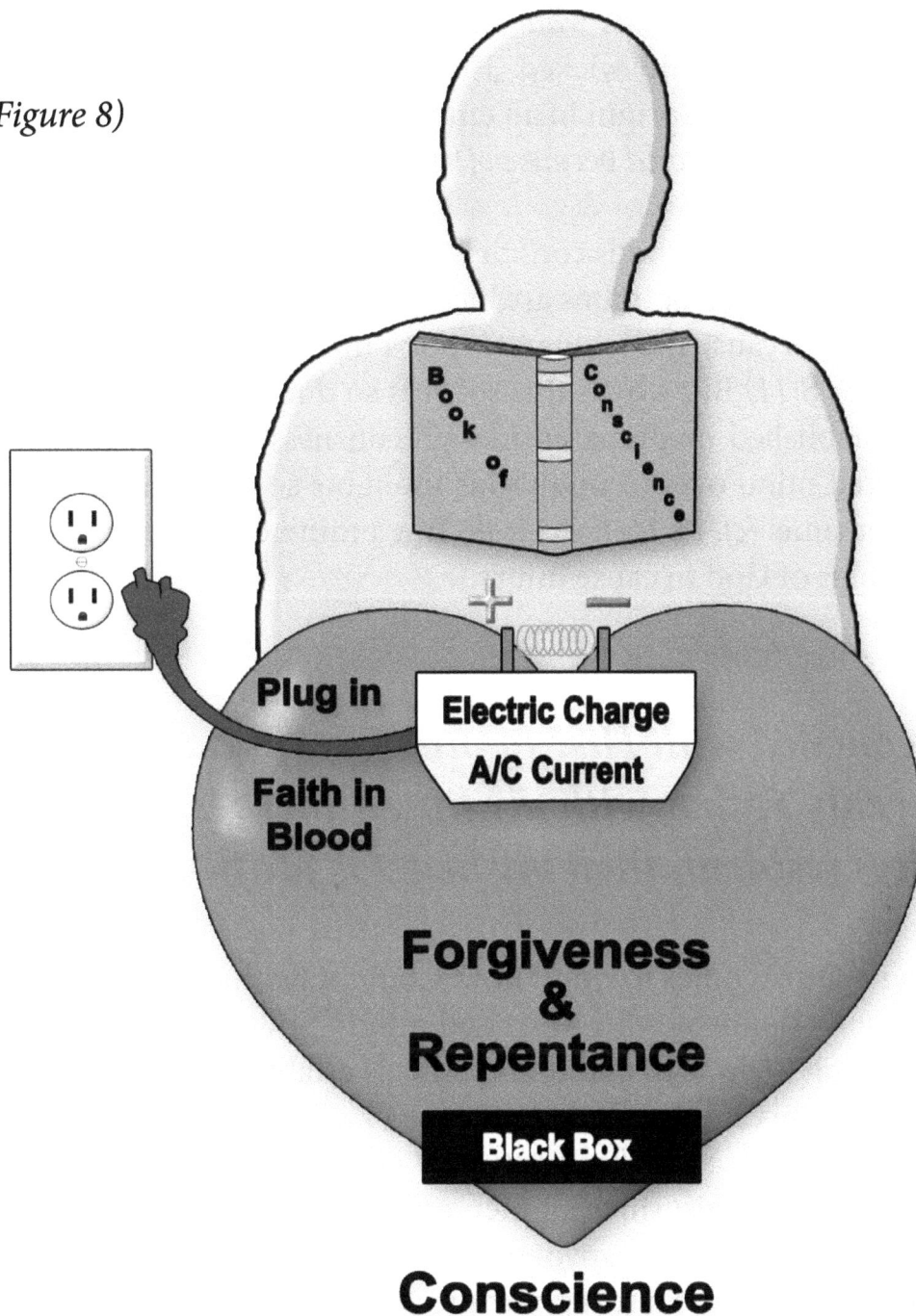

Conscience

Psalms 40:12 AMPC
*"For innumerable evils have compassed me about: **my iniquities have taken such hold on me** that I am not able to look up. They are more than the hair's of my head and **my heart has failed me** and forsaken me." (e.g., Ge 42:28)*

Question: *Who can say that his heart is clean and that he is pure from his iniquity? (cf. Pr 20:9)* Scripture teaches that the heart of a man answers him. *(cf. Pr 27:19)* My concern is *since a man's heart is defiled; just what kind of an answer is heard or given*? You see, the heart of any man is deceitfully wicked. That is, it is filled with iniquities and the smoke trail of each iniquity has its origin in an emotional wound caused by an offense. No wonder Jesus said *woe to the world because of offenses*! *(cf. Mt 18:7)*

Any father who leans on, trusts in and is confident of his own mind and heart is a self-opinionated fool, because his self-opinions are based upon his own lie-based thinking! *(cf. Pr 28:26)* He is a fool because the whole heart of a man is poised to do evil all the time! *(e.g., Pr 6:18; cf. Ec 8:11)* But why is this so? It is so due to the fact that a father's heart has not been established or prepared in righteousness. Hence, Almighty God will give the unprepared mind over to iniquitous thoughts so it may cause a mind to become reprobate over time. *(cf. Pr 16:1; Ro 1:28)* But a mind does not have to be reprobate towards the things of God to cause injury.

⚷

Is my heart reconciled with His? In other words, although I may honor my heavenly Father with my lips, if there is unatoned sin (iniquity) resident, then my heart is far from His!

The thought of being mature comes to mind now. Could it be that a man remains immature so long as iniquity dominates his heart and mind? Now the world's view of being mature has everything to do with adulthood. This is established with certain movies rated for mature audiences only. *This perspective of adult maturity shows mental, emotional, or physical characteristics that are typical of a fully developed adult person.* (Webster's) But my concern is this; since all men carry emotional pain caused by historical traumatic events, how then can anyone say that he or she is mature mentally or emotionally? Surely, Scripture does not support the world's view!

The Apostle Paul said that *"when he was a child, he talked as a child, thought as a child, he reasoned as a child; now that he has become a man, he is done with childish ways and has put them aside."* *(cf. 1 Co 13:11)*

Should you ask anyone to provide you their opinion of what *childlike, childish* or *child* mean, I am sure that they would make statements like, *innocence, immature, purity, inexperienced, adolescent, vulnerable, weak, defenseless,* etc. Assuming that these thoughts are true at least in concept or theory, then let me ask you—was your childhood innocent? Were you not vulnerable to the abuse of adults? If you were to be honest, the only answer you could give is yes! In other words, since offenses and emotional wounds do occur and have existed within the hearts of so many adults, even from their childhood, how can anyone say that to be a child is to be innocent? Lest I be misunderstood, I am not saying that a child is not innocent (as if it were the child's fault), but what I am saying is that as a child the events in that child's life are not innocent. True maturity that is undefiled must be founded upon the Word of God.

Now pertaining to the hearts of the children, Scripture above states that the hearts of the fathers would be turned back to the children as well as the hearts of the children shall be turned back to their fathers. But how is this to be accomplished? Could it be that prior to a certain age of accountability, a young abused child does not have the capacity to formulate or differentiate between a lie and the truth? And should this be the case, then that abused child misinterprets an abusive event or a series of harmful events as masqueraded truth, when it is and always has been a lie to begin with.

Whereas a prophet of God would see the world from or with the perspective of God, in a similar way, Almighty God would have all of humanity to see themselves as they truly are heart wise. In other words, since God looks upon the hearts of all men, shouldn't we also perceive the wounded hearts of others as well as our own? How else shall any man come to know, understand and acknowledge his own iniquity? He can't! So then, before a father can turn his heart back to the children, he first must come to know, understand and acknowledge his iniquities having repented of his offenses towards others and those offenses towards him wherein he has harbored unforgiveness. When he realizes (experientially) that his parents were flawed in their wounded hearts, and that no one of their generation was perfected in their maturity either, then a father will see a pattern of deception which has affected all generations of humanity.

To know, understands and acknowledge your iniquity denotes a personal accountability, does it not? Almighty God would have all men to become accountable with their stuff!

Throughout these past twenty years, I have been asked by many to explain the word iniquity and carnality. I initially was amazed of their ignorance! But in every situation the people have told me bluntly that their pastors never teach on this! It's not just the ordinary Christian either! For I have had many pastors tell me directly that they don't present messages on or about repentance either. They have stated that the people don't want to hear about repentance. I have had many denominational pastors turn and walk away from me or have stated that although I may be scripturally correct, because you are not a Baptist, Nazarene or other, I will not allow you to minister from my pulpit!

To wit, spiritual leadership has disrespected me because of this teaching on repentance! For you see, it is because pastors do not possess any insights on repentance themselves that they have allowed their congregants to stray. The pastors have become brutish (beast-like, carnal)!

Jeremiah 10:21 KJ21
"For the pastors are become brutish, and have not sought the Lord: therefore they shall not prosper and their flocks shall be scattered."

So given the situation today, the apathy within the church exist because a lifestyle of repentance is not appreciated and since it is not appreciated, there has arisen the slow gradual proliferation of humanity's unsuppressed carnality because of our iniquities! For the willingly ignorant, a lifestyle of repentance has become a curse, because such people have chosen to ignore God's Truth! Hence they don't understand God's righteousness!

1 Corinthians 15:34 KJ21
"Awake to righteousness and sin not; for some have not the knowledge of God: I speak this to your shame."

Notes:_____

_____

_____

_____

_____

_____

_____

_____

Notes:_____

_____

_____

_____

_____

_____

_____

_____

_____

_____

_____

_____

_____

_____

_____

_____

_____

_____

_____

_____

Notes:

Epilogue

→ Humility is One of the Keys to the Kingdom ←

Grace is defined and described to be "kindness, favor, pleasant, precious, well-favored, to bend or stoop down to in kindness to an inferior, to bestow, to implore, to move to favor by petition, beseech, deal, to give, in treat, be merciful, have pity upon, make supplication." (Strong's Exhaustive Concordance Hebrew, ref. #2580; p. 430) God's grace is also defined as and described to be, "divine gratuity, free gift, spiritual endowment, religious qualification, deliverance from danger or passion, joy, pleasure, benefit, gift, divine influence upon the heart and its reflections in life." (Strong's Exhaustive Concordance Greek ref.# 5485, 5486; p. 430)

James 4:6-7 NKJV
"God resists the proud but gives grace to the humble. Submit yourself therefore to God, resist the devil and he shall flee from you."

Philippians 2:5-9 AMP
"Let this same attitude and purpose and [humble] mind be in you which was also in Christ Jesus: [Let Him be your example in humility:] Who, although being essentially one with God and in form of God [possessing the fullness of the attributes which make God, God], did not think this equality with God was a thing to be eagerly grasped or retained, But stripped Himself [of all privileges and rightful dignity], so as to assume the guise of a servant (slave), in that He became like men and was born a human being. And after He had appeared in human form, He abased and humbled Himself [still further] and carried His obedience to the extreme death, even the death of the cross! Therefore [because He stooped so low] God has highly exalted Him and has freely bestowed on Him the name that is above every name."

Elohim (Creator God) the Three in One had the very first encounter of satanic devices through , whom Almighty God had created as an inferior spirit. At some point in time, Lucifer's heart became filled with pride. So he attempted to overthrow Elohim once in Heaven. Now this once could represent a season of time in which God might have given grace to Lucifer through His Son Jesus Christ so that he Lucifer might amend his ways for the better. But Scripture bears it out that Satan ultimately refused God and Jesus stated that He saw Satan fall as lightning (from Heaven) to the earth! *(cf. Lu 10:18)* (Interestingly, whenever a space object descends towards the earth, it becomes a ball of fire as it enters the atmosphere.)

It is commonly accepted that Satan (Lucifer) was cast out of Heaven violently as a direct result of God's anger. At least this has been my mind set previously. However, God's Word is true and has been established in the heavens. Therefore based upon the Scriptures above and those that follow, it appears that God Who is Love and through Jesus Christ Who is the expression of humility and not His anger was that very act of violence which resulted in Satan's defeat as the causative factor in his removal from Heaven. I base this on the notion that Almighty God does not need to display His wrath since His wrath would be akin to the wrath of man, which as Scripture points out, does not and never shall fulfill the purposes and intents of Almighty God! *(cf. Jas 1:20)*

Now this concept of the humility of God was birthed out of the fractured relationship that exists between my two children and me. Over the years, my many attempts to reconcile our relationship failed. As their father, I have humbled myself and have tried to convince my kids of my sincerity of heart by stooping down to them in kindness but without their reciprocity. In affect, I have taken the burden of their heart wounds upon myself in hopes that they might reconsider and prefer a renewed relationship with me over the embittered one that currently exists. But I am aware that people may choose to ignore or refuse reconciliation because they prefer to retain or grasp their bitterness as a right or a means of self-sentencing or torment. My only possible notion as to why could be that any display of love actually intimidates others and that humility as an attribute of love's expression will cause people to fear!

Over the years, certain people have told me the following. In Texas, a fellow minister told me directly, that my kindness towards him often intimidated him. He said this because all other contacts and associations that he has had in the past where conditional and self-serving. Even my mother told me that she was intimidated by the friendly people of Texas. She said this because her life experiences were devoid of such kind hearted relationships. And again, during my employ as a law enforcement officer, other officers were intimidated by the demonstration of God's joy that I possessed back then. Even Scripture mentions this to some degree in *Proverbs 25:21-22* wherein we are encouraged to give bread and water to the enemy that is hungry and thirsty. In doing so, we heap coals of fire upon his head. Finally, as Jesus Christ died on the cross, His love was such that it caused the soldiers to be fearful as well! You see, our acts of humility as an attribute of Love shall intimidate our enemies!

8——

My only possible notion as to why could be that any display of love actually intimidates others and that humility as an attribute of love's expression will cause people to fear!

Why does God resist the proud? Because Satan became prideful in his praise position as a created spirit being! Therefore, through the humility of Jesus Christ, Almighty God did face (to bend or stoop down to in kindness to an inferior) Lucifer in Heaven, Almighty God expects each of us to walk humbly ourselves here and now before God and as we do so; our humility will overcome the devil, just as Jesus Christ's humility threw the devil out! Notice: I am not saying that Almighty God is humble, for He would have no reason to be. But what I am stating is, Jesus Christ was humble and that His humility disarmed Satan so much that Satan would have none of it! But why does God resist the proud—whose hearts are filled with the pride of life? Because He confronted prideful Lucifer and He expects each of us to do the same as He! I've since learned that all titillations of sin activate the demonic, while addressing sin agitates the demonic and forgiving offenses disarms the demonic. Please understand that the demonic does not mean demons, but this expression has everything to do with the evil deeds of people.

Could it be even at that time in antiquity, that Jesus Christ spoke to Lucifer saying, Look, there is something wrong here in our relationship! I take full responsibility for your woundedness! Allow Me to help you. Please Lucifer! Allow Me to prove to you My sincerity! Take My grace which is sufficient for you and allow Me to help you overcome this pride of life that emanates from your proud heart! Don't do this to yourself, for why would you die in your sin? Notice please, that if this were the case herein then lays the very first reason for Jesus Christ to die vicariously (substitutionly)! Almighty God has placed the burden of woundedness squarely upon His shoulders through His Son Jesus Christ! Through Jesus, Almighty God entreated (pleaded, beseeched, implored, petitioned) Lucifer as a divine influence upon his heart and its reflections in Lucifer's life! This deferment was Almighty God's appeal to Lucifer to reconsider the evil of his ways, by reconciling his relationship as a recipient of God's grace! This does not imply that all evil activities beyond this point of injury are God's responsibility however. You see, although God does understand, this does not mean to say that He condones our evil ways beyond the point and time of our woundedness! Note: Should this conversation have actually occurred between Almighty God and Lucifer, then just as God took the corrective measures to do the right thing--that is to initiate reconciliation, so to then must each of us take the corrective measures and do the right thing in and throughout the days of our living by way of God's Word of reconciliation! *(cf. 2 Co 5:17~21)*

Herein lays a plausible explanation for the reason and purpose of the grace of God which He has bestowed upon man. Specifically, Almighty God wants to prove to wounded humanity His sincerity of regret (pity) and He does so through all the attributes of His amazing grace, for it is His grace that is sufficient for us as well. Hence, God gives more grace to the humble and in doing so our humility provides us the victory over the pride of heart. God's grace is His divine influence upon our wounded heart and His reflections in and throughout our life! In other words, He alone knows which direction we will choose to follow. Now, the humility of God as seen in His Son Jesus Christ proves to us Almighty God possesses a humble heart and Scripture bears this out in *Philippians 2*, especially! *"Let this same attitude and purpose and [humble] mind be in you which was also in Christ Jesus: [Let Him be your example in humility:] Who, although being essentially one with God and in form of God [possessing the fullness of the attributes which make God, God],"* What is so amazing here is that Almighty God, in essence, is telling us the very same thing He told Lucifer! People, people, people! My heart's desire (which means "of the Father") is to convince you, even persuade you, of My sincerity of love towards you. I really do understand! I take full responsibility for your wounded heart! I must, because you can't! Only please, receive My grace as the evidence of My sincerity! Let Me fix all that is wrong with your heart! Allow Me to remove the affliction of your iniquities and all the lies within the memory content of your conscience, before it is to late! *(cf. Re 20:12-15)*

Now, to demonstrate to you this notion, let me ask you. Ordinarily, someone would perhaps acknowledge his involvement in a wrong or a mishap as an unintended event, right? His feeling of remorse and regret would obligate his involvement thereby confirming his guilt of conscience. Hopefully, his culpability would produce in him a desire to make things right. Is this not so? So, here we have Almighty God, the Creator of all things, in and through Whom all things created consist, are energized, propelled and are sustained. Almighty God is all knowing. He knows ahead of time, because He inhabits eternity. He sees the end from the beginning and knows all things well! Therefore, in light of these truths, it is reasonable too say that the immense love Almighty God has for fallen man obligates Him to make things right so that His mercy can flow!

It is a matter of a more complete understanding, for forgiveness is a composite of so much more than what we presently know! Just as most people consider grace to be solely God's unmerited favor, so likewise do most people think of God's forgiveness as being reduced in importance to something man merely acquires as the recipient of His grace? What must be understood on our part is that according to the original language, forgiveness means "to make things right or to correct a wrong first so that mercy can flow!" In other words, Almighty God in the demonstrated humility of Christ knew things went wrong. So He did what was required to make things right in order that His mercy and grace might flow. His great and awesome love for fallen man and, as an attribute of His amazing grace, obligated God to first address the problem of sin as His divine influence upon our wounded heart and His reflection (evidence or manifestation) of His grace in our life. In other words, God knows the path that we shall take and the consequences of our choices. So, He sent His Son in the fullness of time to make the necessary correction. He made things right first, so that all the benefits of salvation might flow towards fallen man! It is now up to each one of us to acknowledge God's correction and to choose to make things right ourselves.

Philippians 2 states that Jesus Christ did not think this equality with God was a thing to be eagerly grasped or retained. He abased and humbled Himself [still further] and carried His obedience to the extreme death. This statement possesses the heart of God for doing the right thing and making things right, first and foremost as the highest priority of God's throne! Almighty God could have retained his grudge and outrage against Lucifer and fallen man. But He does not! Just as Lucifer had a will to choose righteousness and humility, so too does every man! Therefore, taking the scriptural example of *Philippians 2*, we learn that no man should ever think of his iniquities to be his identity (of his embittered, wounded heart) as something to be grasped and retained! We are to let go of our pride of life and the idolatry within our hearts! The only remedy for this iniquity is humility and forgiveness! As a man is humble and forgives the offenses of others against him, he actually crucifies the propensities of the flesh (the activation and the agitation of demonic activities) which demands only retribution and retaliation! Humility teaches us Heaven's knowledge about forgiveness and it provides us a skill, as that ability to do something well! Humility reminds us that the wrath of man never fulfills the purposes and the desires of God. *(cf. Jas 1:20)*

Based upon the preceding, hopefully you can accept this spiritual truth of power and authority so far as it pertains towards humility. Whereas, arrogance is the opposite of humility, pride of life and the idolatry of the heart oppose the heart of God!

Matthew 16:19 AMPC
"I will give you the keys of the kingdom; and whatever you bind (declare to be im-

proper and unlawful) on earth must be what is already bound in heaven; and whatever you loose (declare lawful) on earth must be what is already loosed in heaven."

1 John 4:18 AMPC
"There is no fear in love [dread does not exist], but full grown (complete, perfect) love turns fear out of doors and expels every trace of terror! For fear brings with it the thought of punishment and [so] he who is afraid has not reached the full maturity of love [is not yet grown into love's complete perfection]."

Why does the Devil flee? Because he is fearful of humility since it is an attribute of love! This means if we are fearful, then we are not truly humble and remain terrified. Look at it this way; whereas faith may be the opposite of fear, humility is that which causes fear to flee! The reason being that humility is one of the keys to the Kingdom, and what a powerful position of authority and power it is! Humility will rout our enemy because it is an attribute of love! Through humility we agree with Almighty God, for there is power in agreement! For as Scriptures asks, how can any two walk together unless they agree? *(cf. Am 3:3)*

Micah 6:8 AMPC
"He has showed you, O man, what is good. And what does the Lord require of you but to do justly, and to love kindness and mercy and to humble yourself and walk humbly with your God?"

Notice that in *Micah 6:8* we read that man is to humble himself and to walk humbly with God. This implies that God is also humble for how shall our humility be consistent with God's humility unless of course Almighty God is first humble Himself? Now, this agreement does not mean to agree with or to condone any evil activity beyond the point of injury. However, it does pertain towards those offenses which preceded the evil activity. But Scripture also states that Jesus Christ even went the extra mile—death on the cross! This implies that God's humility extends beyond the capacity of man's understanding as to why! God's grace towards us is His daily reminder to us of His sincerity of His humble heart to subsidize (promote, back, sponsor, reimburse) our reconciliation!

You see, grace is defined and described to be "kindness, favor, pleasant, precious, well-favored, to bend or stoop down to in kindness to an inferior, to bestow, to implore, to move to favor by petition, beseech, deal, to give, in treat, be merciful, have pity upon, make supplication." (Strong's Exhaustive Concordance Hebrew, ref. #2580; p. 430) God's grace is also defined as and described to be, "divine gratuity, free gift, spiritual endowment, religious qualification, deliverance from danger or passion, joy, pleasure, benefit, gift, divine influence upon the heart and its reflections in life." (Strong's Exhaustive Concordance Greek ref.# 5485, 5486; p. 430)

God Created the Good and the Evil

Isaiah 45:5-7 KJV
"I am the Lord, and there is none else, there is no [other] God besides me: I girded thee, thou though hast not known me: that they may know from the rising of the sun, and from the west, that there is none besides me. I am the Lord, and there is none else. I form the light, and create darkness: I make peace, and create evil: I the Lord do all these things."

Mortifying the Deeds of the Flesh

Romans 8:12-13 AMP
"So then, brethren, we are debtors, but not to the flesh [we are not obligated to our carnal nature], to live [a life ruled by the standards set up by the dictates] of the flesh. For if you live according to [dictates of] the flesh, you will surely die. But if through the power of the Holy Spirit you are [habitually] putting to death (making extinct, deadening) the [evil] deeds prompted by the body, you shall [really and genuinely] live forever."

• Having come this far in this booklet, hopefully you would agree with Scripture that by eradicating lie - based thinking [falsehood] that this deceit is part and parcel to iniquity. You should also appreciate another insight regarding the mortification of the flesh. Typically, the expression to mortify pertains towards a killing, and scripturally speaking this is correct. But in light of our iniquities, as the unatoned sin of our souls, this killing also applies to the elimination of our iniquitous thoughts altogether and this is because you have come to realize, know, understand and acknowledge that what ever iniquity you fail to uncover, the precious blood of Christ shall not cover! After all, the last thing that you would want is to be called a worker of iniquity by Almighty God because of the falsehood which you have practiced in and throughout your living.

The Framework of the Book of Hebrews (Magna Charta)
Script: Descending Order of the Spirit: (Positive)

Scripture tells us that the Chosen People of God lived 430 years under the emotional torment of Egyptian bondage and oppression. Scripture also provides an historical record of those families who were separated and whose families were either enslaved or assailed by the powers that be and imprisoned during the first century. *(cf. Heb 4:8-10)* Present day, the news abounds with those atrocities against humanity by certain despots, who inflict upon and within their victims emotional wounds. Even in marriages, spouses as well as children are victimized by one another imprinting heart felt wounds and this is nothing compared to the wounds the Hebrew People endured for the four plus centuries of Egyptian bondage!

Only please, receive My grace as the evidence of My sincerity! Let Me fix all that is wrong with your heart! Allow Me to remove the affliction of your iniquities and all the lies within the memory content of your conscience, before it is to late!

It appears to me the message of most leading Christian Ministers (such as Kenneth Copeland) and the like preach that forgiveness is just an act of faith and that all one most do is declare it and it is so. I sincerely believe their message to be incorrect although their intentions are sincere for it avoids the deeper issues of the heart! It is true that we all want to be forgiven, is this not so? But without an awareness of our own heart issues and the process of forgiveness, any other declaration of forgiveness would be just lip service. This makes forgiveness a prerequisite of true Christianity! *(cf. Mt 18:34-35, 5:22-26)*

I said that forgiveness has a process. Now who do you know that does not want to be forgiven? Do you want to be forgiven? Your forgiveness is assured when you amend your heart attitudes towards 1) all people who have offended you throughout your life. 2) Forgive those offenses which you have kept within your heart all these many years. Forgiveness is assured when you forgive people (parents, teachers, relatives, friends, business relationships, etc) 3) submit all emotional wounds to the cross since these remain the seed bed of all lie - based thinking (Iniquitous thoughts) which all of us rehearse.

When people embrace forgiveness in each of these three areas, and we repent to Almighty God for harboring such torments then the Truth of God is revealed to our hearts and His deliverance is experienced on a personal level! Now what is wrong with that? Who do you know that does not want to be delivered from their stuff? You should know that God's deliverance is true revival and may be ours to enjoy and retain here and now! It is ours for the asking, but as we ask, we must ask correctly. You see, deep repentance must aspire towards that which caused Jesus Christ to suffer and die. His level of repentance is compared to His broken heart, for it was His heart that was broken. Unless our repentance reaches this depth in love, as that level which Jesus Christ possessed on the cross, then our repentance should be suspect!

The other thing to consider is that once your forgiveness extends towards those unforgiven offenses, unforgiven people and unsubmitted emotional wounds, then your faith becomes God's faith and it is no longer fear based! This is so because we have leaned our entire personality upon God's mercy and goodness. Did you know that fear is the opposite of faith? When we apply forgiveness towards Offenses, People and Emotional Wounds, our faith is no longer defiled or corrupted. If there were ever a time to wallow in your stuff, this is it! Now is the time and today is the day of salvation! This is the time to stir yourself up, agitating your heart issues, in order to deal with them once and for all so that you would be set free of all their torments! If you don't, then you will continue to self sentence yourself to your bondage!

Another thing to consider in this process of forgiveness has everything to do with Life's Values! In other words, when people live their values and have not forgiven Offenses, People and have not submitted their Emotional Wounds to Jesus Christ, their value system is wrong or at the very least very unhealthy. Because of unforgiveness, people retain bad or inappropriate relationships (unhealthy soul ties) and align themselves to various associations (parties, denominations, clubs, religions, gangs, etc.) to satisfy an inappropriate need. They have become need based, for it is convenient to satisfy their fleshly cravings which exist to further enslave them via the reinforcement of wrong motives! *(e.g., Lu 18:1-8)*

On the contrary however, since we have forgiven Offenses, People and have Submitted our Emotional Wounds to Christ, who died just as much for these and them as He did for you and me, then our Life Values are properly aligned with a pure conscience towards the things of God. The result being: Seasons of Stability are lived, Satisfaction and Fulfillment is experienced, and, No Negative Emotions are tied to our Memories! *(cf. Heb 4:12)* Circumcised Heart (Flesh in Emotional Realm), Rest of God is Entered *(cf. Heb 4:3)* to know the Lord, a wounded heart is no longer the connector between the Soul and Spirit, Soul and Spirit finally separated baring their own hearts. The Soul's Heart is Healed and the Spirit's Heart is One with God's, because between the spheres of the Soul & Spirit hangs the plum line of the Word of God to measure all behavior, and finally, behavior now indicates the soul heart's condition of true circumcision!

At this point, the Holy Spirit opens deeper Truth and Revelation to our hearts, for as Scripture states, *God hates the proud but He gives more grace* (Truth and Revelation) *to the humble. (cf. Jas 4:6-7)* You see, God's grace is multi-faceted just as God is, for His amazing grace coexists with Him. And because our humility is an expression of His love that is shed abroad in our hearts by the Holy Ghost, the Anointing of God becomes evident in every area of our lives! This anointing is not only to be anointed for this or that, but it is that anointing which validates God's calling on your life!

We no longer remain Cross Minded, but at this point we become Throne Conscious! *(cf. Heb 4:18)* This new priority is the Glory Realm of God, for it is here that Signs, Wonders and Miracles occur! And the reason that these occur is because the anointing has ushered us into the office and calling of the Apostolic and the Prophetic authority! Look at it this way. Allow the apostolic to be the father of the church and the prophetic to be the mother of the church. Because of these two offices, the intended harvest is ours and that in every area of life. Now, as this harvest comes to us; we no longer have to seek after it! Isn't this wonderful? This harvest is acquired not with wrong motives, but with proper motives since our life adheres to Christ in faith believing.

This harvest will be like a magnet for others who desire the same blessings. Just as you have become magnetized, your magnetism will draw others to you. This therefore establishes the ministry of evangelism which is the presentation of the Glad Tidings (Good News) of the Gospel of Truth! It is here that the five fold ministries of the church are founded because pastors and teachers are needed to unify the church!

■ Closing Thoughts ■

The Letter of the Law/ the Spirit of the Law

Psalms 119:4 KJV
"Thou hast commanded us to keep thy precepts diligently."

Psalms 119:15 KJV
"I will meditate in thy precepts, and have respect unto thy ways."

Psalms 119:27 AMPC
"Make me to understand the way of thy precepts: so shall I talk of the wondrous works."

(Hebrew Concordance #6485 Pik-kood)

Mandate for of the Law, Commandment, Statute

In these few verses I notice that the precept of God is not the way of God! Although, His precepts can lead us to the mannerism or intent (way) of the Law, it is obvious to me that the precept of God carries with it the lifestyle to live as in His Ways. Just as the founding fathers of these United States of America wrote the Declaration of Independence and the Bill of Rights as the Statute of the land, Almighty God has written His Mandates that are the Commands to the Universe and as such these commands are the inalienable rights of people! *(Hebrew Concordance #1869 derek [deh-rek])*

Applying this notion of the command to Repent then, I can see God's carry over intention as His way to live as a lifestyle of repentance and not just a command to repent. You see, God's way is like a road map upon which you and I make travel as the seasons of our individual lives unfold. And it is because of the precept that His way is realized and lived.

So in closing, suffice it too say that what hearing is to the ear, listening is to heart! And what the precepts of God are to His Law, so likewise are the Ways of God to a lifestyle of repentance! In this is found the Letter of the Law as His Precepts and the Spirit of the Law as His Ways.

Notes:_____
_____
_____
_____
_____
_____
_____
_____
_____
_____
_____
_____
_____
_____
_____
_____
_____
_____
_____
_____

Notes:_____

_____

_____

_____

_____

_____

_____

_____

_____

_____

_____

_____

_____

_____

_____

_____

_____

_____

_____

_____

Addendum

<u>The word INIQUITY found 278 times</u>

Genesis 15:16; 19:15; 44:16

Exodus 20:5; 28:38, 43; 34:7-9

Leviticus 5:1, 17; 7:18; 10:17; 17:16; 18:25; 19:8; 20:17-19; 22:16; 26:39-43

Numbers 5:15, 31; 14:18-19; 15:31; 18:1, 23; 23:21; 30:15

Deuteronomy 5:9; 19:15; 32:4

Joshua 22:17-20

1 Samuel 3:13-14; 15:23; 20:1, 8; 25:24

2 Samuel 7:14; 14:9, 32; 19:19; 22:24; 24:10

1 Chronicles 21:8

2 Chronicles 19:7

Nehemiah 4:5

Job 4:8; 5:16; 6:29-30; 7:21; 10:6, 14; 11:6, 14-17; 15:5, 16; 20:27; 21:19; 22:23; 31:3, 11, 28, 33; 33:9; 34:8-10, 22, 32; 36:10, 21-23

Psalms 5:5; 6:8; 7:3; 7:14; 14:4; 18:23; 25:11; 28:3; 31:10; 32:2, 5; 36:2-3, 12; 37:1; 38:18; 39:11; 41:6; 49:5; 51:2-5; 53:1-4; 55:3; 56:7; 59:2; 64:2; 66:18; 69:27; 78:38; 85:2; 89:32; 92:7-9; 94:4, 16, 20-23; 106:6, 43; 107:42; 109:14; 119:3, 133; 125:3-5; 141:4-9

Proverbs 10:29; 16:6; 19:28; 21:15; 22:8

Ecclesiastes 3:16

Isaiah 1:4, 13; 5:18; 6:7; 13:11; 14:21; 22:14; 26:21; 27:9; 29:20; 30:13; 31:2; 32:6; 33:24; 40:2; 53:6; 57:17; 59:3-7; 64:9

Jeremiah 2:5, 22; 3:13; 9:5; 13:22; 14:10, 20; 16:10, 17-18; 18:23; 25:12; 30:14-15; 31:30-34; 32:18; 33:8; 36:3, 31; 50:20; 51:6

Lamentations 2:14; 4:6, 22

Ezekiel 3:18-20; 4:4-6, 17; 7:13-19; 9:9; 14:3-10; 16:49; 18:8, 17-30; 21:23-29; 28:15-18; 29:16; 33:6-18; 35:5; 39:23; 44:10-12

Daniel 9:5, 24

Hosea 4:8; 5:5; 6:8; 7:1; 8:13; 9:7-9; 10:9-13; 12:8-11; 13:12; 14:1-2

Micah 2:1; 3:10; 7:18

Habakkuk 1:3, 13; 2:12

Zephaniah 3:5, 13

Zechariah 3:4-9

Malachi 2:6

Matthew 7:23; 13:41; 23:28; 24:12

Luke 13:27

Acts 1:18; 8:23

Romans 6:19

1 Corinthians 13:6

2 Thessalonians 2:7

2 Timothy 2:19

Titus 2:14

Addendum

Hebrews 1:9

James 3:6

2 Peter 1:9

The word INIQUITIES found 56 times

Leviticus 16:21-22; 26:39

Numbers 14:34

Ezra 9:6-13

Nehemiah 9:2

Job 13:23-26; 22:5

Psalms 38:4; 40:12; 51:9; 64:6; 65:3; 79:8; 90:8; 103:3-10; 107:17; 130:3-8

Proverbs 5:22

Isaiah 43:24; 50:1; 53:5, 11; 59:2, 12; 64:6-7; 65:7

Jeremiah 5:25; 11:10; 14:7; 33:8

Lamentations 4:13, 5:7

Ezekiel 24:23; 28:18

Daniel 4:27; 9:13

Amos 3:2

Micah 7:19

Acts 3:26

Addendum

Romans 4:7

Hebrews 8:12; 10:17

Revelations 18:5

About the Author

Brother Ed Marr is an ordained lay-minister and published author. He is a graduate of Calvary Cathedral International Bible School in Fort Worth, Texas. Almighty God has groomed Ed as one of His Prophets (Right Reverend) to preach and teach Repentance as a true indicator of his authenticity as a true Prophet of God.

Lamentations 2:14 "Your prophets have predicted for you falsehood and delusion and foolish things. And they have not exposed your iniquity and guilt, to avert your captivity [by causing you to repent]; but they have divined and declared to you false and deceptive prophecies, worthless and misleading."

He is a retired California Highway Patrol Officer. His law enforcement career has taught him specific investigative skills, specifically the necessity for the economy of words. Ed's style of writing reflects this bare bones investigative technique. Prior to this, he served 7 years in the United States Marine Corps. His notable duties were as a Marine Security Guard (Saudi Arabia & Saigon) and a Drill Instructor (San Diego, Ca.)

God has used Ed throughout his law enforcement career. During his twelve year employment as a State Traffic Officer, Brother Ed experienced angelic visitations in his patrol car as well as at collisions. At crime scenes, Officer Marr has had demonic encounters, and as a uniform officer, hundreds have accepted salvation through the ministry Almighty God has called him to. Over the past thirty years, Brother Ed has experienced the power of prevailing prayer in that 3 people have been raised from the dead, and powerful creative miracles have occurred as a direct and immediate result of prayers of faith! Brother Ed has taught repentance to the prisoners at the Okmulgee County Jail where he was able to test the message of repentance, where frequently he received spontaneous standing ovations!

Ed believes that it is just a matter of time before the pulpits of America will open the doors to him and this NOW WORD of and about Repentance.

"Mister" Ed (as he is often called) is not another cookie cutter preacher who parrots others. His disposition is laid back, and his presentations are subdued. The very power of righteous words makes the impact, penetrating hearts, decimating carnality. *(cf. Job 6:25)* Although a big man with a big voice, Ed does not rely upon these physical attributes to impress. Rather, he permits the fire power of The Word to express itself in truth!

While residing in Fort Worth, Texas, a specific prophetic word was spoken to Ed in January 1997, and the time has come for its fruition. That prophetic word is:

"My son, I call you my champion! Just as David slew Goliath, you too shall slay the giants of this land! I have placed that champion inside you; even your physical size is no accident! I have made you a giant on the inside and out. Men will know that you are my champion, because the Sword of the Spirit shall be in your hands and My words will come forth from your lips. Your light will shine bright in the land and it will drive out the darkness that resides in the hearts of carnal men! Therefore, rejoice My son, for I will be at your side just as I was with David!"

Presently, Brother Ed resides in Coweta, Oklahoma,
and he is available for field ministry. You may contact him at:

(918)574-5139
email : *bigedvocal@gmail.com*

Enjoy these other great books from Bold Truth Publishing

Seemed Good to THE HOLY GHOST
Daryl P Holloman

Effective Prison Ministries
Wayne W. Sanders

Obedience is Not an Option
Brian Ohse

TURN OFF THE STEW
Judy Spencer

The Holy Spirit SPEAKS Expressly
Elizabeth Pruitt Sloan

Matthew 4:4 - Man shall not live by bread alone...
Rick McKnight

VICTIM TO VICTOR THE CHOICE IS YOURS
Rachel V. Jeffries

SEEING BEYOND
Kelly Taylor Nutt

SPIRITUAL BIRTHING - Bringing God's Plans & Purposes and Manifestation
Lynn Whitlock Jones

BECOMING PERFECT - Let The Perfector Perfect His Work In You
Sally Stokes Weiesnbach

FIVE SMOOTH STONES
Aaron Jones

KINGDOM of LIGHT 1 - kingdom of darkness - Truth about Spiritual Warfare
Michael R. Hicks

WISE OLE OWL - The Language of Heaven-ease
Marcella O'Banion Burnes

Available at Select Bookstores and at
www.BoldTruthPublishing.com

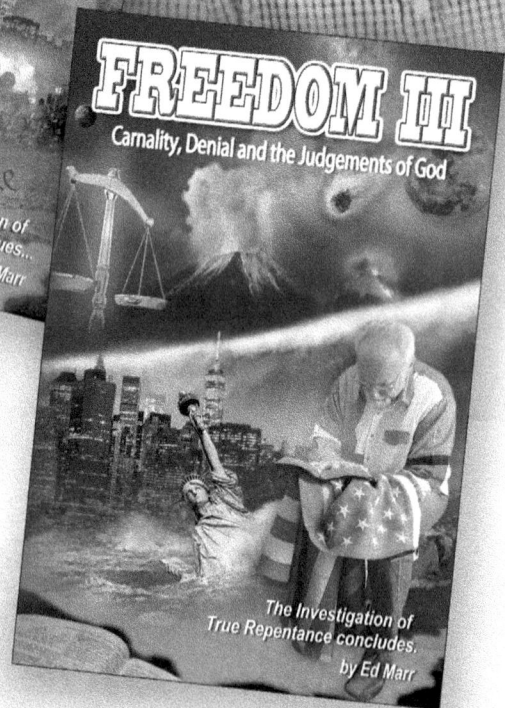

www.ingramcontent.com/pod-product-compliance
Lightning Source LLC
Chambersburg PA
CBHW080510110426
42742CB00017B/3060